RAMONES AT 40

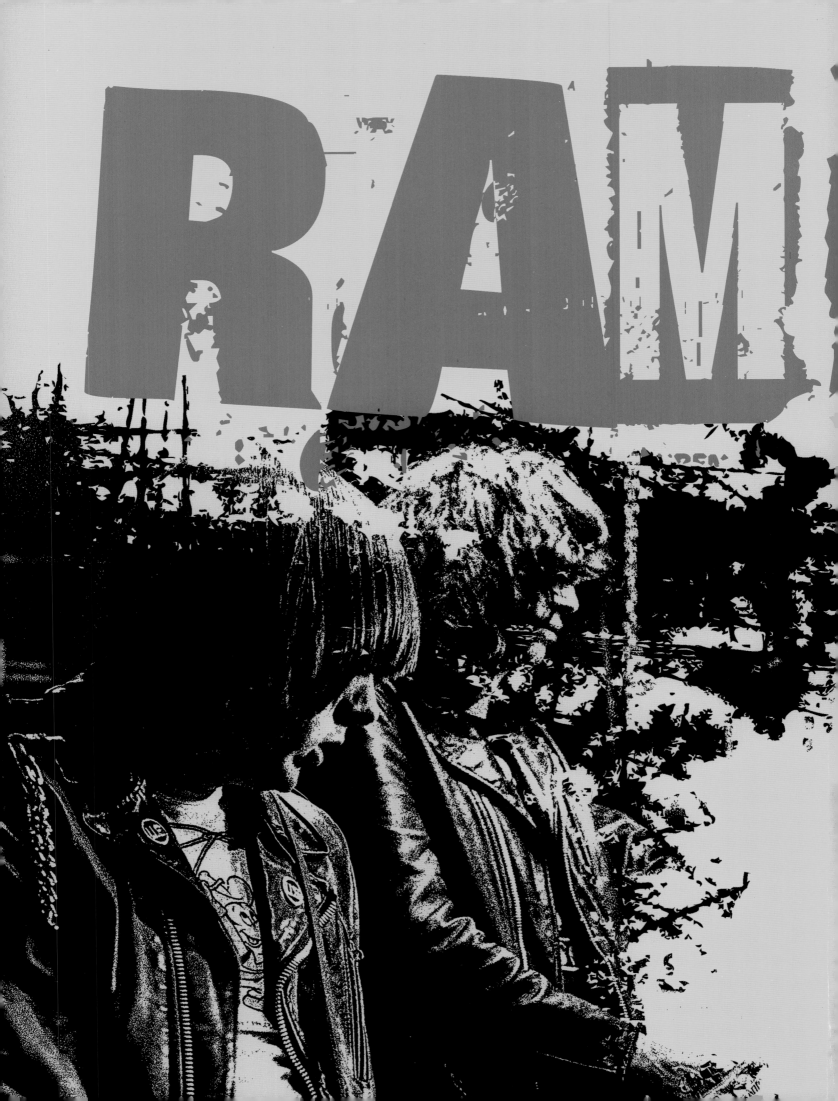

RAMONES AT 40

MARTIN POPOFF

FOREWORD BY CJ RAMONE

STERLING
New York

STERLING
New York

An Imprint of Sterling Publishing
1166 Avenue of the Americas
New York, NY 10036

ISBN 978-1-4549-1834-9

Distributed in Canada by Sterling Publishing
c/o Canadian Manda Group, 664 Annette Street
Toronto, Ontario, Canada M6S 2C8
Distributed in the United Kingdom by GMC Distribution Services
Castle Place, 166 High Street, Lewes, East Sussex, England BN7 1XU
Distributed in Australia by Capricorn Link (Australia) Pty. Ltd.
P.O. Box 704, Windsor, NSW 2756, Australia

For information about custom editions, special sales,
and premium and corporate purchases, please contact Sterling
Special Sales at 800-805-5489 or specialsales@sterlingpublishing.com.

Designed by Paul Palmer-Edwards, Grade Design

Manufactured in China

2   4   6   8   10   9   7   5   3   1

www.sterlingpublishing.com

Contents

FOREWORD

It was 1976, 200 years since the United States of America won its independence and fought its way to becoming a star on the world's stage. Rock 'n' roll was our gift to the world, catching on like a wildfire through the '50s and the '60s all over the planet. But by the '70s it had become a bloated, virtuoso-filled business of elitists.

And then it happened.

Four misfits from Forest Hills, Queens, borrowing from the greatest rock 'n' roll bands of the '50s, the bubble-gum and pop from the '60s, and the proto-punk bands like the Stooges and the New York Dolls, created a stripped-down hybrid that caught everyone off guard.

Taking their name from an alias used by Paul McCartney, the Ramones started a revolution that changed music forever when they released their first record in February 1976. Although it took years for them to be recognized for their genius, they inspired entire genres of music and almost every band that came after them.

Like a lot of kids, many of my firsts were had listening to the Ramones. In the summer of '77 I met a pretty blonde girl who took me back to her house, pulled out a record, put it on the turntable, and held the cover up. "You ever heard the Ramones?" she asked. It was the first record and I was mesmerized as soon as "Blitzkrieg Bop" kicked off. I had my first kiss with that pretty blonde girl that day and smoked my first joint. It was a rite of passage for me.

Years later when I was in the band, I told Johnny that story. "You know how many times I've heard stories like that, CJ?" he responded. I found out later how true that was after I had been in the band for a few years and young fans would recount their experiences to me. That was one of the most important lessons Johnny taught me: the fans come before everything. "We're nothing without them" was how he said it. He always took time to talk to the fans and genuinely cared about them. He was tough and unflinchingly honest, which did not win him any popularity contests, but I appreciated his directness and respected him for it. He was my mentor.

Joey was Johnny's polar opposite. He was quiet and and had a keen sense of humor. I had a lot of laughs with Joey. We went to shows together and spent a lot of time listening to music at his apartment and talking about everything imaginable. Joey was my friend.

Dee Dee was always my favorite. One of the greatest rock 'n' roll songwriters of all time and the absolute undisputed originator of punk rock style. I got to play with him in the Ramainz and was lucky enough to have some good times with him. Although he did threaten me on a couple of occasions!

Tommy was the mastermind. The Ramones were his creation. The look, the sound, even who played what instrument, it was all him. Johnny told me that so you can bet it's true. He was a natural and only started playing the drums because he could not find a drummer that could play what he heard in his head. Every punk rock drummer owes what they do to him, directly or indirectly.

I was there for the Ramones most successful last years until we retired. Although it was time for us to go, I always hoped for the reunion call. Instead I got the calls that I didn't want. First Joey, then Dee Dee, then Johnny, and finally Tommy.

Since they are gone, I've tried hard to carry the standard and to help keep the fires burning. The Ramones' music started a revolution forty years ago that still lives today and we are all part of it! RAMONES FOREVER!!!

CJ RAMONE, October 2015

01

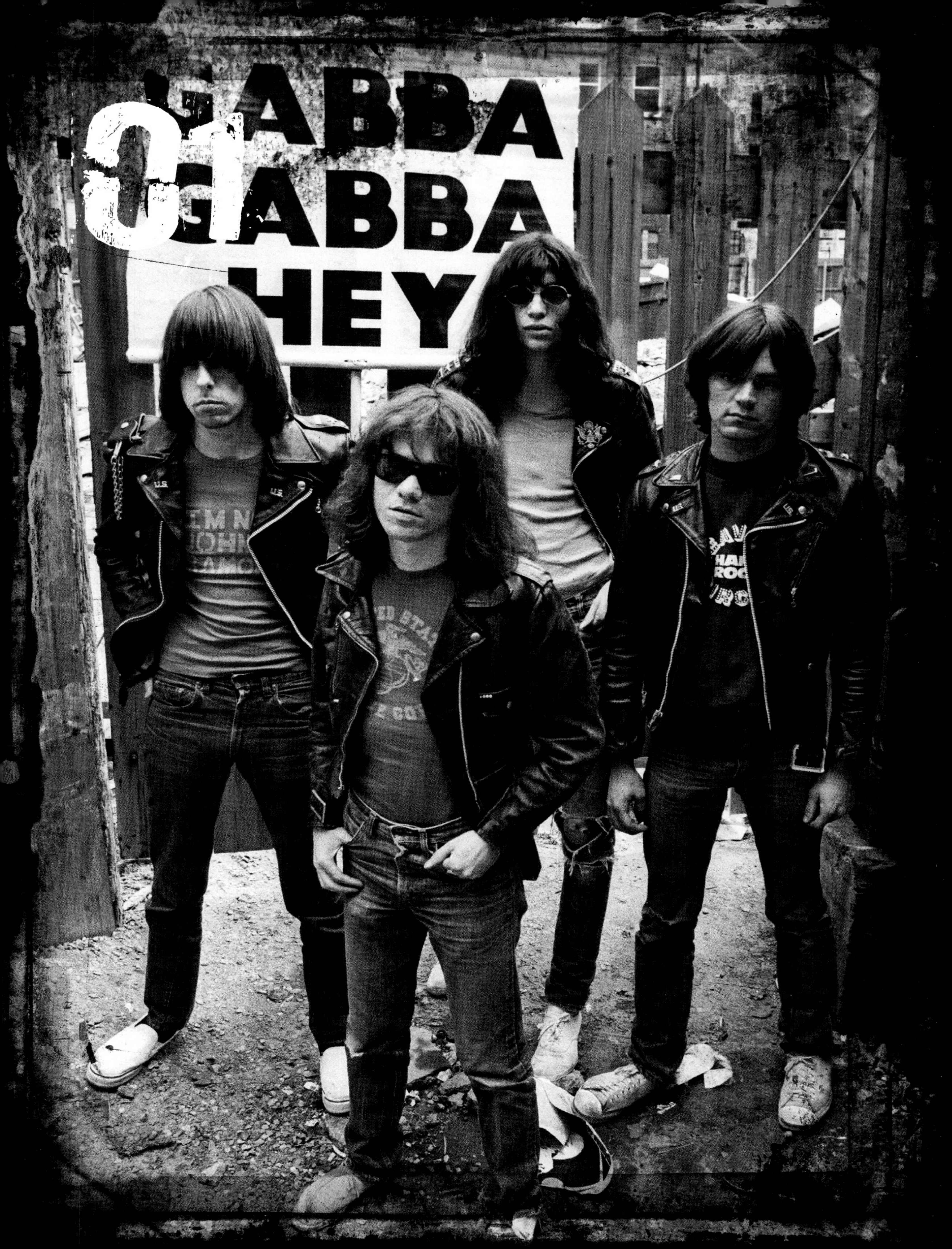

1974-1975

"A BUNCH OF DEGENERATE WEIRDOS HANGING OUT"

"A BUNCH OF DEGENERATE WEIRDOS HANGING OUT"

Awkward.

It's a word that comes up time and again when friends and collaborators of Joey, Johnny, Dee Dee, and Tommy—a.k.a. the Ramones, muse over the "Greek tragedy" that is this band's bite an' claw through life towards deification in death.

Awkward describes the individual—and even more so, the composite, collective, and clashed—upbringings of the original band. Other words that spring to mind are: ragged, sad, occasionally bucolic, and mostly misfitting. But fortunately for the world the Ramones also embody—in just the right measured doses—a love for forms of rock 'n' roll that are complicated and nonobvious for brats from Queens, New York.

For when the Ramones parachuted into Lower Manhattan in the mid-1970s, a rock revolution erupted—one that at its heart mirrored the interior and quietly desperate lives of its revolutionaries. Within two years it would widely be known as punk rock, and the Ramones would be credited for its blitzkrieg birthing.

Punk would come to mean many things, and the Ramones would embody some of them and not others. But it would always be a club of containment, a club for the awkward and the misfits, the introspective and the bullied. A club whose membership, while remaining select, became global as the Ramones and the Pistols ignited the fires of fans across New York, London, and, eventually, the world.

Despite being the acknowledged fire-starters, the Ramones only took their rightful place as cultural icons with the rise of the next punk wave in the '90s. Sure, Joey, Johnny, Dee Dee, and Tommy would live to see some of their rich legacy celebrated. Yet, the end would ultimately mirror the beginning, the Ramones trading the psychological warfare and dysfunctional families of their childhoods for much the same style and intensity of strife among themselves.

Life for each of the boys began in contrasting colorful situations that were far from perfect, even though there would be more episodes of traditional familial fun than any of them would ever see once they donned the leather jacket—none of the Ramones, save for CJ, would ever have kids.

PAGE 8: The band had their look honed by the time this portrait was taken in 1977.

OPPOSITE: Dee Dee—the "true" punk of the band. Photographed by Roberta Bayley in 1976.

"GENE VINCENT HAD A VERY STRONG IMAGE IN THE SENSE THAT HE WAS ROCK 'N' ROLL, AND NOT JUST GENE VINCENT. I MEAN, ELVIS PRESLEY OR LITTLE RICHARD, THERE WAS MORE TO THEM THAN JUST MUSIC. IT BURST OUT OF THEM; THEY WERE PURE ROCK 'N' ROLL. MUSIC OF THAT TIME, I WAS A LITTLE KID AND I USED TO LISTEN TO THE RADIO AND WHEN YOU HEARD THOSE SONGS, MAN, THEY BURNED LIKE A FIRE. THOSE GUYS REALLY HAD IT; THERE WAS SOMETHING THERE."

TOMMY RAMONE TO RALPH ALFONSO, *CRASH 'N' BURN NEWS*, 1977

Doug "Dee Dee Ramone" Colvin had it worst. Born September 18, 1951, in Fort Lee, Virginia, the family soon decamped for a US military base in Pirmasens, Germany, where his army dad drank heavily and scrapped relentlessly with his German mom at all hours. A failure at school, the young Dee Dee retreated into the fantasy world of horror movies, while also discovering Bill Haley and nascent rock 'n' roll at an early age, one of the more meaningful gifts given to him by his mother.

Dee Dee's first introduction to the mystery of the guitar was via a school bully, back in Germany, named Krudd. This discovery, alongside the pervasive influence of Elvis (who had been stationed in Germany) and the invasion of the teenage mind that was the Beatles, had Dee Dee thinking that rock 'n' roll was the only way forward for a teenage screw-up like himself. Even at age twelve, his idea was to try to win enough money at the bingo games to buy a guitar.

Instead, he spent his last days in Germany (now in Berlin, an upgrade from the bleak industrial and military no-man's-land of Pirmasens) shop-lifting and hiding from his father. In between these activities, he was also busy listening to Armed Forces Radio,

dreaming his way through the earliest teen magazines, and catching early rock 'n' roll bands live at the Berlin American High School and the Liverpool Loop. As part of a transformation of which he was in dire need, Doug became Dee Dee—a persona inspired by a *Playboy* article on wrestler Gorgeous George's reinvention of himself as a character.

With his parents soon to divorce, the already nomadic Dee Dee, his sister, Beverly, and his mother, Tony, fled Germany to the Forest Hills area of Queens, New York in 1966. Pretty quickly, Dee Dee was on the streets of Manhattan at its most shockingly crumbled, scoring—Dee Dee had already discovered injectable morphine in Germany—hustling, dealing, and finally finding a couple of future Ramones, who were at this point named John Cummings and Tommy Erdelyi. Work in the mail room of an insurance company added some normalcy in a life that tended to be governed by acid, pot, heroin, clubbing, and lurking around the less salubrious parts of Central Park. After one too many intense fights with his mom, Dee Dee moved to the city, finding an apartment at 85th Street and Second Avenue. He also managed to get himself a car, an old Volkswagen, and the party continued.

OPPOSITE, TOP: Gene Vincent (second from left), with the Beatles (John Lennon to his left, George Harrison to his right, and original drummer Pete Best at far right), at the Star Club, Hamburg in 1962. Vincent, along with Jerry Lee Lewis and even Johnny Cash, were pioneers of the bad boy rocker sort, essentially, in spirit, the first punks.

OPPOSITE, BOTTOM: Elvis Presley at Ray Barracks in Friedberg, Hesse on March 1, 1960. By the time Presley returned from military duty, rock had moved onto its "British invasion" phase. Soon the Stones and the Kinks would join the Beatles in representing musical groups as gangs. The Ramones, really only one rock 'n' roll generation past the Beatles, would take this image to its logical conclusion.

ABOVE: The accepted narrative is that the apocryphal Beatles moment was their appearance on the *Ed Sullivan Show*. However, shows in Germany, particularly around Hamburg, were inspirational milestones as well.

PROTO-PUNK TRINITY: MC5, THE STOOGES, AND THE NEW YORK DOLLS

Although the Ramones have been known to cite a bewildering array of influences ranging from '50s rock, the Beatles, the Who, Herman's Hermits, girl groups, garage rock, a bit of psych, and then even further outliers (although strangely nothing too, too heavy metal), the guys regularly came to consensus around the value in their lives imbued by the Stooges, MC5, and the New York Dolls.

To the Ramones, and many others, knowing that music was a secret handshake in a rarefied club. In fact, Dee Dee says that that's how they met, with the proverbial, "I heard you liked the Stooges." If you did, you had to be friends because everybody else hated them. And then Joey, who called the Stooges "an exorcism, a total release," said that, despite the gulf in their personalities, seeing the MC5 and the Stooges live cemented his relationship with Johnny.

The Stooges were denigrated not only by many of the Ramones' peers, but also by the industry at this time. "The Stooges weren't very well organized," explained manager of both the Stooges and the Ramones, Danny Fields, to journalist Ralph Alfonso back in 1977. "They had a lot of problems that had no relationship to what they were doing, like drugs, criminality, a general sort of unproductive karma about them. Musically, they were brilliant, but professionally they weren't quite together like these boys are. There's a big difference. It's ironic, you know, when the Stooges needed all this support, there was no one around to give it to them."

"They came up with the revolutionary idea of going back to the basics, and

ABOVE: Iggy Pop and the Stooges, San Francisco, 1974. Notes Ralph Alfonso, on a conversation he had with Stooges and Ramones manager Danny Fields, "The Ramones were way more together and were way more focused. That was the Stooges' problem—they weren't focused. . . . The Ramones learned very carefully from their heroes, sort of where they failed and how they could channel that forward."

they were too premature and too unorganized to do it," noted Tommy. "But now it seems to be building again, and if it's well-organized and well-planned, there's certainly a need for a band with raw energy, excitement and good songs. It's gotta come from the inside. You can't construct it, you can't put it together—it's gotta burst forth. That's what we love, man; that's the kind of feel we have. That is rock in our opinion, just the feel, the essence of it, the pure energy."

The similarities between the birthing of the Stooges' sound and that of the Ramones are striking. When I asked Stooges' guitarist Ron Asheton about the band's seminal self-titled debut from 1969, the record that arguably planted the seed for punk, he told me, "It was probably that way, at least for me, due to ignorance of my instrument. I had to play simple because I was just learning how to play. So I just picked up, you know, those three chords. When I go back now and talk to people like Thurston Moore and Mark Arm, they're going, 'We learned to play guitar from that record because it seemed like it was accessible to us. We could actually sit down and figure it out and get some joy out of it. Wow, I can play!' And that's pretty much sheer bravado, about being young upstarts, if you will, that it was just an extension of our personalities, like anybody who plays, actually. Just our attitude. We hung out together all the time, doing everything together, so I guess that's what came out. When you put four minds together in a bad situation, they might turn into a killer. But you put four minds together in a nice musical situation, and something good is going to come out of it."

Similarly Michael Davis, bassist for MC5, told me his band's credo: "Our music is really based on fundamentals. Our records weren't full of production techniques and trickery or illusions of anything, synthesizer machines, or whatever. We based our music on the fundamentals of blues and rock 'n' roll, very basic stuff. And when you come right down to it, that's always good; it always works."

Once MC5 were gone, the Ramones escaped boredom by heading out in Tommy's car to go and see the New York Dolls, who, at the time, became a more immediate inspiration for the band—not to mention being the first exciting

New York band since the Velvet Underground. While Joey was citing their decadence, their energy, and their great songs, Johnny was looking directly at guitarist Johnny Thunders, thinking, hey, I could do that.

"I think we really would have gotten to that point that they described later on as punk or new wave," Dolls' guitarist Syl Sylvain told me, having been asked about what the future would have held had they stayed together. One must remember that the Dolls, through their visit to the UK, are considered one of the prime inspirations that sparked the UK punk scene. "That's what we were working on. We were the first ones to really bring that out from the bands that we were inspired by, which were the girl groups from the '60s—the Shangri-Las, of course, and the Ronettes. Don't forget, we used to do 'Give Her a Great Big Kiss.'"

"The Dolls were just a fucking train wreck about to happen, and that's why we died," concludes Syl. "And we were really deep too. We had something to say for our generation. We were complaining because we didn't like what was going on. We didn't like the Vietnam War. We didn't like the big stadium rock concerts where you had to bring your damn magnifying glass to see the fucking rock stars. We didn't want tons and tons and tons of guitars and drums, and this and that, and singing 'Wooohooaaahhh!' We wanted a couple of chords, really quick, a great drum beat—give me the song in two minutes and get the fuck out of there. And that's what we helped invent. We didn't even know it, but basically our frustration at not getting satisfied in other things is how the New York Dolls got birthed. Johnny didn't want to play 'Frankenstein' because he thought there were too many chords. Poor Johnny, more than three chords for him was like, 'Oh, I gotta go back to school.' I'm like, 'Johnny, don't worry about it. Every progression, it comes back again, so there are six chords but it's over and over again. Once you get to six chords it's easy.'"

BELOW: Joey Ramone's first band was very much influenced by the New York Dolls, pictured onstage in 1974. Andy Shernoff remembers, "Joey was six foot seven wearing platforms."

Thomas "Tommy Ramone" Erdelyi was born January 29, 1949, in Budapest, Hungary, the Jewish son of Holocaust survivors. By the age of six, he and his family had relocated to Forest Hills, Queens. Scarred by being bullied as a teenager, Tommy (self-styled as Scotty, at first—like Dee Dee—he reveled in the idea of a pseudonym) battled with anxiety. Andy Shernoff recalls, "Tommy was a shy guy. Very unassuming. He couldn't handle Johnny making fun of him. He couldn't handle . . . he was a little neurotic. I think he had some anxiety, because he used to live . . . for a while about two blocks away from me. I would see him around and he used to pop pills to deal with people; he had anxiety. I don't know what disorder he had. I never asked him. He would just tell me, he would say people made him nervous, so he had some kind of disorder along that line." Still, he was soon playing garage rock with a classmate—the future Johnny Ramone. In an interview with Mark Prindle, Tommy later recalled, "I was in a band called Tangerine Puppets with him. He was on bass at that time though. I was the guitar player. He was amazing! Because he was playing bass, he was free to really move around. He held his bass really high up like a machine gun, and he would use it like a machine gun. He'd go all over the stage aiming it at people. He put on a very exciting show."

Tommy and Johnny drifted apart, with Johnny later contacting Tommy and telling him that he was now playing with Dee Dee, who he had befriended over their mutual appreciation of the Stooges.

John "Johnny Ramone" Cummings, also of Forest Hills, was born in Long Island, October 8, 1948. The only son of a construction worker, Johnny was a natural at baseball and would become a lifelong fan of the game, particularly rooting for the New York Yankees. "He's a person filled with a lot of energy," commented Tommy. "A lot of energy, maybe a little anger. He wanted to be a baseball player, a pitcher. And whenever he played, he'd throw a lot of fastballs. But he's

a complex character; that's the best way I can describe it."

Johnny was also a huge rock fan, instantly gravitating toward the Stooges, MC5, and later Slade and the New York Dolls. The guys were also at this time, together and separately, partaking enthusiastically of glam fashion, including the platform boots, the satin pants, and the meticulously teased hair. Unsure what to do with his life, Johnny attended military school and was all set to go to college in Florida when he suddenly turned around and returned to New York. He had two main goals: first to try and act less like a delinquent, and second, to become a rock 'n' roller—by his own admission, the college ruse had been more of a draft dodge anyway. Progress was not instant, with Johnny delivering dry cleaning and working for his dad as a plumber. Soon though, he slid into petty crime, and ended up on welfare—all before the Ramones would come together under the tutelage of natural leader Tommy.

"Three of us used to hang out in Russell Sage; it's a junior high school," said Johnny, speaking with *Punk* magazine's John Holmstrom in March 1976. "We used to play stickball and things like that. You know, I used to play a lot. Diamond; do you know how to play diamond? We'd play sick games too; steal the old lady's underwear or something. Pull people across the lines. We used to go to the World's Fair. We lived right near the park. Yeah, we saw all the rock concerts there. We used to be vandals. We used to rip TVs off the roof and throw 'em down into the street. We used to go around and throw rocks and bottles through people's windows. We used to walk around and do that all day every day." He adds to Ralph Alfonso in 1977, "Our background, we're a bunch of degenerate weirdos, that's all. We were a bunch of degenerate weirdos hanging out in Forest Hills when we should've been looking for a decent job or decent careers. But we were hanging out listening to records instead and all kinds of nasty things. I guess that's where the Ramones came from."

OPPOSITE, TOP LEFT: Tommy Ramone at the Roundhouse, London in 1976: "It was strange, because as soon as I started playing drums, things seemed to click. Right away we had what became the Ramones sound. I guess it was the missing ingredient. Before I started playing, the sound was choppy, and with me playing it became smooth and driving."

OPPOSITE, TOP RIGHT: According to Andy Shernoff, "Johnny controlled the business stuff; he kept a record of every show, and he was always checking on the box office. He thought the only way they could really make money is if they kept their expenses down." Johnny shows off his guitar skills here at CBGB in 1976.

ABOVE: The Ramones' former rock 'n' roll high school in Forest Hills, photographed in 2008.

"If you notice, kids used to really go and hang out," added Dee Dee in the same interview. "Sometimes we used to do different things, go to Flushing Meadow Park. When John went to school, kids used to come up to him and say, 'Can we buy some stuff off you?' And he'd actually never smoked any of that stuff in his life. They used to have those peace demonstrations and stuff, and I used to heckle the demonstrators."

The band, speaking with Ralph Alfonso of *Cheap Thrills* in 1977, remembered how their school days shaped them. Tommy recalled, "Forest Hills High School was twenty-fifth in the ranking of the best schools in the United States; 86 percent of the kids who went to Forest Hills High School went to college, which is really a high number. To drop out of Forest Hills High School was, you know, 'dropping out;' you are committing suicide. You just don't do that! I mean, unless you had an academic diploma, forget it!"

"I felt like an outcast, as if I was just passing, you know, getting by," added Johnny. "I liked high school. I went every day. I didn't miss one day of high school."

"I hated it," countered Dee Dee. "I never used to go until I dropped out and then I used to go there sometimes when I was lonely, to see some of my friends."

Our last of the beloved original Ramones, Jeffrey Ross "Joey Ramone" Hyman was born on May 19, 1951, in Manhattan, and, like the others, grew up in Forest Hills, Queens. Always sickly, Joey wound up tall; he was six foot three, frail, and socially awkward, and at age eighteen checked himself into the hospital for severe obsessive-compulsive disorder. For Joey, it had actually been touch and go right from the beginning. He had been born with a baseball-sized tumor attached to his spine due to a condition called sacrococcygeal teratoma. Risky, high-level surgery to remove it was a success, but neurological damage down the road was always a possibility. Indeed his eyesight deteriorated even as a child

and he was behind in his reading skills throughout school.

"I grew up in Queens, New York, in all different areas," Joey told *Hit Parader* in 1981. "I never really liked Queens, but that's where I grew up. I was an outcast. That's how the Ramones came to be—we were all outcasts. We all lived in the same area in Forest Hills and we didn't have any friends because everyone thought we were odd, I guess. It wasn't that *they* didn't like *us*, though; *we* didn't like *them*. They were all a bunch of assholes. You just didn't want to have anything to do with them. They were real straight and creepy."

Like Tommy, Joey was bullied, and like Tommy, he would rise above it and carve an identity for himself, taking on the character of the sullen rebel. His brother Mickey would be a constant in his life, although at times the relationship was strained. A loner and artistic, Joey was very affected by the divorce of his mother Charlotte from his father, Noel, when he was eight. Noel headed up a trucking company, and was by some accounts an oppressive presence over Charlotte and the kids. There would be a new stepfather, but a car crash later widowed Charlotte, to whom Joey always stayed close.

"Our parents got divorced when we were very young," explains Joey's brother Mickey Leigh, "so that was the beginning of our delinquent youth where we spent a lot of time unsupervised; let's put it that way. Don't get me wrong, my mom and dad loved us very much and did their best—it could've been much worse—but I guess we were emotionally injured. Music was medicine."

Shy at school, Joey replaced jocular friendship with an interest in TV and rock 'n' roll. As far as playing went, he dabbled with the accordion before moving on to the drums at thirteen. Charlotte, who was now running an art gallery, encouraged both Joey and Mickey with their musical endeavors, and indeed Mickey also became a lifelong guitarist, bandmember, and solid songwriter.

"Joey always was supportive," says Mickey. "We had our ups and downs, but

"JOHNNY WENT TO MILITARY SCHOOL FOR HIGH SCHOOL OR SOMETHING, AND HIS FATHER WAS A CONSTRUCTION WORKER, CONSERVATIVE, DISCIPLINED. AND HERE'S JOEY, HIS MOTHER WAS AN ARTIST, HE'D SIT THERE DOING WEIRD PAINTINGS. THEY WERE DIFFERENT PEOPLE WITH DIFFERENT BACKGROUNDS AND DIFFERENT GOALS, WHO ENDED UP IN THE SAME BAND."

DICTATORS' BASSIST, ANDY SHERNOFF

that was more about things like when I helped him with his music. He was always very encouraging when we were getting along well. I know he was always very proud of me and he did convey that to many of his friends, who told me that he used to brag about me all the time. And we did collaborate a lot. There's actually a record we made together called *Sibling Rivalry*."

Joey, like Dee Dee, dropped out of high school (Tommy and Johnny finished their studies), and became, of all things, a hippie. Mickey, indeed, speaks of Joey's migration to Greenwich Village, walking around in bare feet, taking the pilgrimage to San Francisco, and then supporting himself back in New York by handing out flyers and selling plastic flowers.

Kicked out of the house by Charlotte's new boyfriend, Joey nonetheless helped at his mother's gallery, at times sleeping there overnight, shielding the window with strategic placements of large paintings for privacy. Without a proper job, Joey, like Johnny, also ended up on welfare, but eventually landed a role in a hard glam band called Sniper, serving as a flamboyant David Bowie-inspired lead singer with

the stage name Jeff Starship. It was a transformation that impressed brother Mickey so much that he was sure Joey would rise above his health problems and the OCD, which the family had been told would debilitate him for life.

"Joey had very, very bad OCD," explains Ramones friend and collaborator until the end Andy Shernoff of the Dictators, in our interview of April 2015. "He'd walk down the street and walk off the curb or he'd walk around the pole. He would switch things around in the apartments. A half-empty coffee cup would be in the same spot over days or weeks. But to me, Joey was the sweetest guy in the world as far as

ABOVE: *Sibling Rivalry* was a three-track CD EP issued by Alternative Tentacles on October 11, 1994. Producer credits across the tracks go to Joe Blaney, Ed Stasium, Daniel Rey, and Andy Shernoff.

OPPOSITE: Left to right: *Punk* magazine's Legs McNeil, Andy Shernoff from the Dictators, and an unnamed friend at CBGB in 1977.

"I KNEW THAT PUNK ROCK WAS ON THE WAY. BUT WE WERE NEVER REALLY LIKE THE RAMONES, ALTHOUGH WE HAD A LOT IN COMMON. WE DID INFLUENCE THEM TO WEAR THEIR LEATHER JACKETS, BECAUSE WE WERE THE FIRST. WE HAD THE ALBUM OUT FIRST, AND WE DID 'CALIFORNIA SUN' FIRST, SO WE PRE-DATED PUNK ROCK, CBGB'S PUNK ROCK AS WE KNOW IT, ALL THOSE BANDS. AT ONE POINT IN NEW YORK, THERE WERE ONLY THREE BANDS WITH RECORD CONTRACTS: US, KISS AND THE NEW YORK DOLLS, AND THEY CAME BEFORE US BY A COUPLE YEARS."

DICTATORS' GUITARIST, ROSS THE BOSS

I was concerned. I can't remember me having any kind of disagreement with him. He might've had his quirks, but I never had any incidents with him. My interaction with Joey was that this guy's the best friend you could ever want."

Tommy concurred, "He was obsessive-compulsive and he was also quiet and shy. Then slowly he came out of his shell. But his main problem was the OCD. It was inconvenient because he would always be straggling behind because he had to do certain repetitive things. So it was very inconvenient actually. It was time-consuming to have to deal with it. But we didn't know what it was. We just thought he was neurotic, actually."

Through Sniper, Dee Dee met Joey and was soon crashing in the gallery, too. Mickey had also been in Tangerine Puppets with Johnny and Tommy, so suddenly the four of them were all connected. Tommy had been pressing Johnny for two years to start a new band, and Joey later recalled that it was at this point that Johnny (who had just lost his job) and Dee Dee decided they wanted to form a band with Joey (who had been just kicked out of Sniper on account of his gawkiness), even though Johnny was initially hesitant, sizing up Joey as a hippie freak.

"There was also another person who didn't quite make the band—Richie Stern, who was also a very interesting, colorful individual," Tommy remembered. "Yeah, I wanted to put a band together with quirky, interesting personalities, some people who were intense and talented, and slightly different. I just thought they would be perfect for a rock band. At the time, it was like the glam/glitter kinda scene, right? So basically, initially, it was just to be part of that scene. But as soon as I started working with them, it became fairly evident early on that they were coming up with very interesting songs like I've never heard before. And so we tried to channel that into something creative. So that was a huge plus—the fact that they were so creative at writing songs. That was part of the band's structure, the fact that they came with a lot of baggage from their past, whatever that might have been. It fueled the intensity of the band, I think."

"Tommy was a visionary," muses Shernoff. "He saw these guys and said, Johnny could be a rock star, Joey is a weirdo, writes great songs, and Dee Dee is a weirdo, writes great songs. He put them in order, told them where to stand, told them how to dress, produced the first two records. They couldn't have done it without Tommy. Couldn't have done it without Dee Dee, but also Johnny and Joey. Those four guys. You even take Ringo out of the picture . . . you need a Ringo not just for his personality, but for the way Ringo plays drums and gets that band swinging. . . . He's the perfect drummer for the Beatles. And Tommy was very simple on the drums. When the Ramones formed, it was Keith Moon, it was Carl Palmer, all these technical drummers. Here's Tommy keeping the beat, no frills, going from the high hat to the ride, and creating this sound that really changed rock 'n' roll. So many people were influenced by the Ramones."

But at the start Tommy wasn't the drummer. That was Joey's perch, with Tommy beginning as Warhol-inspired kingmaker-cum-ersatz manager, watching and arranging. Johnny wanted Joey away from the drums, saying he couldn't keep up and he took forever setting up his drums. Drummers were auditioned, but they all played too fancy. "Joey didn't have the energy," says Shernoff. "Joey was not very strong physically. But Tommy saw that, hey, Joey's got a great voice, he can't play drums, he's interesting looking, get him out front. Tommy went back there and learned how to play drums."

"Joey was the original drummer and Tommy was sort of the producer/organizer of it," confirmed Roberta Bayley, door gal at cult music club CBGB and photographer of choice for the cover of the first Ramones album, when I interviewed her in March 2015. "But pretty quickly, Johnny became the leader and the decision-maker, for better or worse.

(continued on page 29)

RAMONES

with -BLONDIE- at

MOTHERS

267 West 23rd Street   at eighth ave.

FRIDAY THRU SUNDAY
SHOWS AT 11:00 & 1:00

OCT. 3, 4, 5.

924-9780

I LEFT MY HEART ON CBGB: THE RAMONES AND OMFUG

Rock's ebbs and flows over time are well documented, including swings between the USA and the UK, and then L.A. to New York (to Minneapolis, Seattle . . .). Drilling down to New York City in the '70s, a shift of sorts had taken place from the folk scene of the gentrified Greenwich Village to a more electric situation in keeping with the hard times that the city had been going through, focusing on the Lower East Side, the East Village, and the Bowery. It is hard to believe now, but downtown was emptying of its middle class—leaving crime, grime, abandoned buildings, old forgotten drunks, drugs, and gangs. In this habitat sprung up a new bohemian creative class living on the razor's edge, where most creativity usually gets cut to shape.

Hilly Kristal's CBGB opened in 1973 at 315 Bowery, at the east end of Bleecker Street. The sign read "CBGB OMFUG," which stood for Country, Bluegrass, Blues, and Other Music for Uplifting Gormandizers—a tag more Frank Zappa than Buck Owens that reflected Kristal's admiration for original music, the more idiosyncratic the better.

A youth revolution quickly took over the place, and the likes of Suicide, the Fast, Mink Deville, the Shirts, the Heartbreakers, Wayne County, the Dead Boys, Richard Hell and the Voidoids, Blondie, Talking Heads, the Dictators, Television, and Patti Smith soon came to comprise what was an undefinable sound set. Another outlier among outliers was the Ramones, who arguably are wrapped up in the legend of the place more than any other band

"There wasn't a lot of choice for bands to play in New York City at that time," reflects CBGB employee Roberta Bayley. "Most places wanted cover bands or Top 40 bands. So for bands that wanted to play original music, the choices were extremely limited. And people would be searching all the time, walking around trying to find what crummy bar they could convince to let them play, so they could get their act together and get a little more professional by playing in front of audiences."

"And so the guys in Television had stumbled across this CBGB. It had been Hilly's on the Bowery before that. Hilly wanted to have performances there but his idea was nothing to do with punk rock, which didn't exist really then. But their manager convinced Hilly that if the guys from Television played on Sunday night, they would get the word out and people would come down, and they would buy drinks. What harm could there be? That's how it started. Television was playing on Sunday night, and then the Ramones were one of the earlier bands to play there. The stakes were not very high, because there wasn't really any payment at the beginning. Whatever was collected off the door would go directly to the band. So it was really just a place to have a live rehearsal. Little by little it attracted all the different people who were in bands, which was the main audience. So, in those early days, it was like a clubhouse. They had a little ad in the *Village Voice,* so some people just stumbled in, but mostly it was friends of friends, or other bands."

"People really responded in a positive way to the Ramones, unless they weren't prepared for it. And when the name of the Ramones and the name of CBGB got out there, the club started to attract what we would call celebrity slumming, because the buzz was on about CBs. Paul Simon came down, Ray Davies came down. I remember that Linda Ronstadt came down one time and sat pretty near the front, and I think she was a little shocked and ran out quickly. It was really pretty intense. But the people that had the courage to sit in the front when the Ramones were playing that loud, they liked it."

You read that right—people sat. "Yeah, it was shocking to me too, to realize that, because I worked the door. The door of the club was as far away from the stage as you could get. The stage was way in the back, and even further back after they took the pool table out. But people sat at tables. The original idea was to try desperately to enforce the two-drink minimum, which was pretty difficult to do. But once the club got crowded, which was more around '75–'76, and then started to sell out—the legal capacity was something like 120 people and there'd be probably 300 or 400 people at the club. I was always happy to be sitting by the door, so if anything went wrong, I could run out."

"There wasn't a lot of distance between the stage at CBGB and the crowd," adds Lenny Kaye, Patti Smith guitarist and key rock historian of this seminal scene. "So you would walk off the stage and you would be among your friends. Or you'd be watching your friends on stage. The nice thing about the East Village is that you'd see everybody around. You'd get a sense of who they were and it was very neighborly. CBs was your local hangout, and you'd go down there, and sometimes you wouldn't even see the bands that were on. You're hanging out in front with friends, or having a beer by the bar. It was about as casual—especially in the early days—as could be. And it gave everybody space to grow into who they wanted to be, and who they would become."

TOP: "Country, Bluegrass, Blues, and Other Music for Uplifting Gormandizers."

MIDDLE: Review clips strategically added to a June 1975 concert notice. Rock journalists were instantly "getting it" even if the particular charms of the Ramones totality would be a hard sell to the masses.

BOTTOM: A typical night at CBGB—this was a gig by the Ramones in July 1977.

"I MOVED TO NEW YORK IN '76 OR '77, AND I IMMEDIATELY WENT
TO CBGB. TALKING HEADS WERE PLAYING THERE; YOU HAD A GUY
WHO PLAYED ACOUSTIC GUITAR, GIRL PLAYING BASS, DRUMS—
IT WAS NOTHING. AND NOBODY IN THE CROWD. AND I MET A GUY
[CHARLIE] WHO WAS DOING THE SOUND. . . . . I HAD NO MONEY AT
THE TIME, NOTHING, AND CHARLIE USED TO LET ME BASICALLY
LIVE THERE. . . . . THEY HAD A GUY COOKING FOOD, AND SO I KIND
OF DEPENDED ON CBGB FOR STAYING ALIVE. BUT BY DOING THAT,
I SAW EVERYBODY. AC/DC, WHEN THEY PLAYED THE PALLADIUM,
AFTER THAT, THEY CAME DOWNTOWN AND PLAYED CBGB. BOWIE
WOULD COME, FRANK ZAPPA, ROBERT FRIPP, AND I STARTED
PLAYING WITH ALL THESE BANDS. SO I WATCHED IT GROW FROM
THIS STRANGE, VERY SMALL BAR TO THIS ICONIC PLACE."

RAMONES PRODUCER, BILL LASWELL

He had a military aspect to his mind and was very serious about success and the rules that they were going to go by and the kind of music they were going to play. He had a vision. But I think musically, Tommy fleshed it out and was important to how they developed musically."

The Ramones' first gig is considered to be a showcase of sorts on March 30, 1974, at a space on 20th Street in New York's Flatiron District that Tommy and future Ramones road warrior and tour manager, Monte Melnick, had an interest in, to a crowd of thirty or so. The band played as a trio, with Johnny on guitar, Joey on drums and vocals, and Dee Dee on bass and vocals. Bayley recalled in our interview, "The Ramones had this place where Tommy worked called Performance Studios, and I guess it was like the

rehearsal spot. That was the first place I saw them play. They had a showcase, so I remember seeing them. One time Debbie Harry was there, and I was there with Richard Hell. It was just a local thing. They'd just invite their friends down, to just sort of get some licks in."

Before Tommy took over on the drums, an interim situation found the band with their first of two Richards. "We had two guitar players, me and Dee Dee, and Ritchie Ramone on bass," explained Johnny to John Holmstrom in an interview for *Punk* in March 1976. "But he never played anything in his life! He couldn't keep up. Then it was just us three but we were only rehearsing about once a week. We weren't getting nothing done, really. Just fooling around, just a hobby."

RAMONE

"To them, it was just a hobby," added Tommy. "To me it was an avant-garde thing. Then we started getting really good and I said, 'This isn't avant-garde, this is commercial!' And that's when I started playing drums. When I saw the dollar signs. It changed the whole sound of the group into the way it is now, you know, hard rock."

The first proper show, with the classic band lineup, would be at CBGB on August 16, 1974, to a crowd of—as Johnny remembered it—two people, one of which was Suicide's Alan Vega, who was surprised to see Sniper's glam vocalist Jeff Starship radically transformed into Joey Ramone. The songs were short, simple, shocking, and, arguably, elusively and/or variously "ironic." The Ramones'

"uniform" was also beginning taking shape. Tommy later explained, "What happened was that we wore different things from our teens. We knew each other growing up for a period of years when we were teens ourselves. So we took what was the best individual stuff that we wore over the years that would fit the music. And we did wear all those things. Not necessarily at the same time, but we put 'em together in a way that was comfortable, suited the music and that's what it was. It wasn't an overnight thing. It evolved over a short period."

The band would play out the year as CBGB regulars, becoming the house band of sorts, Dee Dee in particular learning as he went, looking anxiously toward Johnny for direction. To his credit, as Dee Dee reduced the

ABOVE: The heroes of our story circa 1976 photographed by Roberta Bayley.

frequency of bum notes, he would become the most animated and codified "punk" in the band. But at this juncture it was Joey with his fist pumps, hip swivels, kicks, and splayed chicken legs who was the visual center of the presentation. More gigs would take place at Performance Studios, continuing into 1975, when again, CBGB would comprise most of the band's gig itinerary for that year, plus the odd other New York venue and one show in Waterbury, Connecticut.

Significantly, however, the band would play Arturo Vega's loft on February 3, 1975, kicking off a collaboration with the visionary graphic artist that would do as much to make the Ramones iconic, as would their records.

"I saw them rehearse in that loft," recalls Sire Records' Craig Leon in our interview, "and also at Performance Studio. But there was a big backdrop that Arturo had designed that said 'RAMONES' in black-and-white. It didn't have the eagle on it or anything. Just like cutout letters. And I remember it was actually on a blanket, like on a sheet. In any case, they rehearsed there, and Tommy and I got to be friendly, and I bought into his concept of what the band was all about."

Already anointed the band's resident-for-life "art director," Vega helped kickstart their career, as when Craig Leon saw their look and heard them play at Vega's loft, he knew there was something special about them. Leon instigated the band getting signed and then took on the task of producing their seminal record—widely regarded as the first punk album of all time.

1976-
1977

"THE ANTITHESIS OF EVERYTHING"

"THE ANTITHESIS OF EVERYTHING"

For most Ramones' fans, nothing can "beat on the brat" like the band's first three albums, namely: *Ramones, Leave Home*, and *Rocket to Russia*. Each one churned into wondrous being by the sacrosanct original band, now sadly all gone.

The period starting in January 1976 is considered by some to represent the birth of punk; just over a year later, the underground London magazine *International Times* (*IT*) famously announced on its February 6, 1977 cover that "PUNK IS DEAD." And really, only the Ramones offered a significant album during that first eleven months. Only two

weeks after the *IT* cover, the Damned added their voices to the fray (*Damned, Damned, Damned*, released February 18), followed by the Clash (*The Clash*, April 8), and the Sex Pistols (*Never Mind the Bollocks, Here's the Sex Pistols*, October 27), along with two more albums from the heroes of our tale.

Lacking the venom and anarchic call to violence of UK punk, but heavier than all the other New York punk bands, Joey, Johnny, Dee Dee, and Tommy flew the flag prolifically stateside for simple, guitar-centric punk. In doing so, the Ramones came to symbolize punk in truest form, with rock history

PAGE 32: Ready to leave home. The Ramones leave New York to take their music on the road. This photograph was taken on May 19, 1977 to promote their *Leave Home* US tour.

OPPOSITE: The three albums that made the Ramones immortal punk legends: *Ramones, Leave Home*, and *Rocket to Russia*.

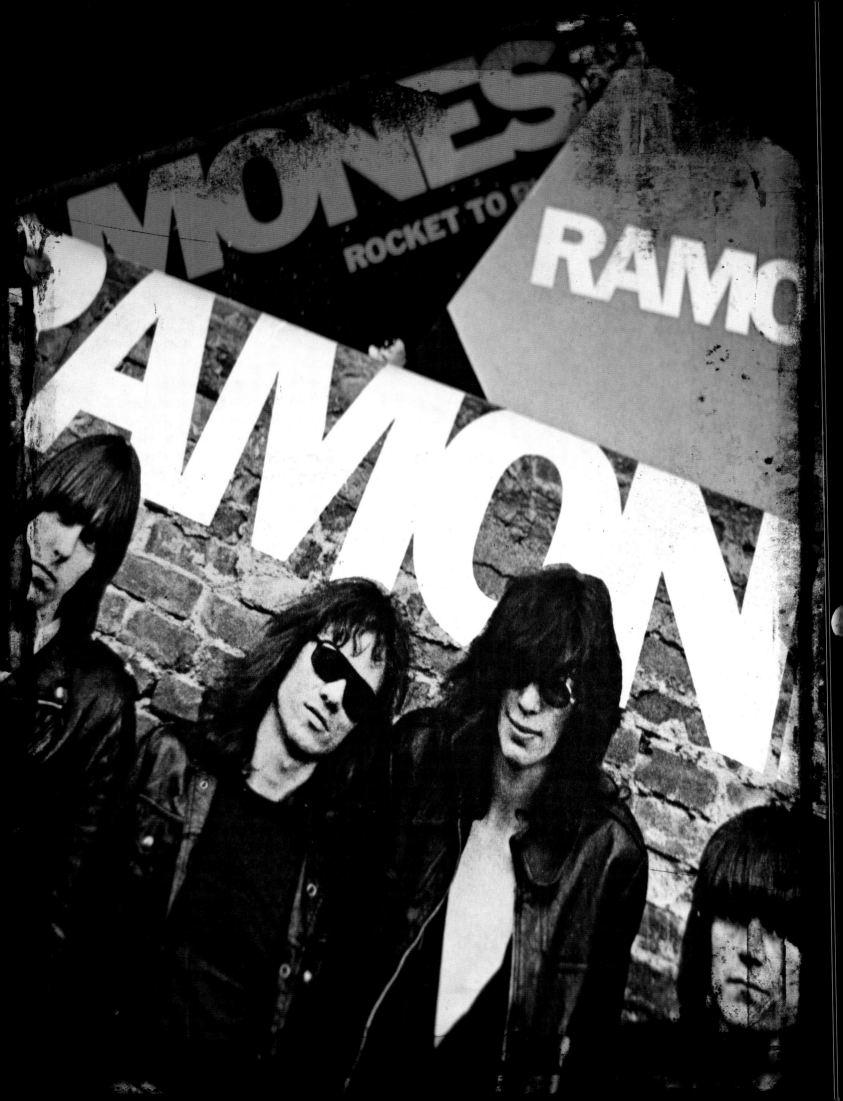

exalting each and all of the trinity of classics the band created during 1976 and 1977 as three of the defining punk records of all time.

Before 1975, Sire Records hadn't been on anyone's radar, proto-punk or otherwise. But the feisty imprint, with its burnt yellow label and stark blue logo, would soon become home for the Talking Heads, the Dead Boys, and, most iconic of all, the Ramones.

During the course of our interview for this book, Craig Leon, part of the A&R team at Sire (run by Seymour and Linda Stein) and producer of the Ramones' first record, explains, "It was a label of primarily European artists who didn't have record deals in America, and Sire released them. And we made a bit of a transformation because the New York scene was starting to look interesting, including things that might be a little more progressive in terms of mental attitude. We figured we might be able to do it the other way around: take something from New York and get a record deal or licensing deal for it in Europe."

"Craig Leon is the one who got us signed, single-handed," said Tommy interviewed in 1976 for *Punk*. "He brought down the vice president and all these people; he's the only hip one at the company. He risked his career to get us on the label!"

"The first time I'd kind of officially brought them to Sire was in '75, when they played with the Talking Heads opening at CBGB," Leon continues. "That's when I went to Seymour and said, let's sign them, and you should sign the Talking Heads as well. Tommy had come from a visual background as well as music. He studied film and, to some degree, he studied recording engineering. His idea was to make this tongue-in-cheek super pop group that was the antithesis of everything else that was going on at that time, very streamlined with these two-minute songs, no guitar solos, where everything was in strict rhythm and everything was going to be 200 beats per minute. And they were all going to look the same. It was patterned after the Bay City Rollers in a weird kind of way, which was one of their

favorite bands, as was Herman's Hermits to some extent—that was Joey's favorite band."

However, neither Craig nor Seymour were too fond of the band's early demos, although there was definitely a buzz around the band because of the Ramones' live show. Steve Paul and Blue Sky Records were interested, as was Marty Thau (on the management front), but not so much Marty's associate David Krebs, who had worked with gender-bending shock rockers the New York Dolls and was now busy with Aerosmith and Ted Nugent. In the end, Danny Fields became their manager, declaring that the Ramones had "changed his life."

"He'd come down to see us a lot, and gradually we became closer," explained Johnny during the same *Punk* interview. "He'd help us out a lot before he became our manager, you know, give us advice. We'd tell him we needed a manager and he kept telling us to hold off. Finally we decided we had to find one and we asked him."

Fields' first management move, according to Craig Leon, scored dividends: "What actually cemented the deal was that he got Linda involved, who was Seymour's wife, obviously, to become the co-manager of the band. And when that happened, Seymour pushed the button and signed them. But it wasn't like he had a St. Paul moment, an epiphany. The process of bringing them into the label had taken quite a while."

On being asked what he originally liked about the band, Leon responds, "Rock 'n' roll had gotten a little bit boring at that time, and the Ramones were different. They weren't studied like the Eagles. They were back to what I grew up on, and what they grew up on, and a lot of people grew up on, an amalgamation of old rock 'n' roll—Link Wray, Eddie Cochran, loud guitars, a bit of something that was dangerous—combined with great pre-Beatles kind of pop, like the Ronettes and the Shangri-Las. And the attitude was very, very New York. And I thought that they were really funny—I loved their lyrics—and I thought anything that's really funny these days,

because New York was so grim, would be something that would be interesting to get involved with."

"They were loud, but they weren't that loud because they couldn't afford big amplifiers," Leon continues. "They had these little Mike Matthews' amps, which later on were augmented with bigger ones. They were energetic and pretty fierce, but live, the whole thing would be one long song. Everything would run together and stop only when they were completely exhausted, or they had a fight about what song they were going to do next. One of the main problems on the record was getting songs to start and stop."

So, with label and management in place, it was off to work getting history down on record. Leon recalls, "The studio we used was called Plaza Sound, which was the old NBC Symphony studios on top of Radio City Music Hall. It was a large, cavernous building, about the size of Abbey Road One over here in London. It had a big pipe organ in the middle of the room, along one wall. And it was on a floor above Radio City, where they also had the rehearsal halls for various bands like orchestras and also the Rockettes, the dance troupe, downstairs. There was a relatively small control room, small for the size of this big room, but it was pretty much state-of-the-art for its time. It had a couple of delays, but nothing much in terms of outboard gear. It had a great desk, an old API desk, and a 3M™ machine and a good array of mics and everything, they were nice people that ran it, good engineers. So we used it a lot at Sire, late at night, because we didn't have a lot of money at the label. This is way before the big corporate people bought into Sire. Everything was on a shoestring budget."

As for capturing Joey's voice, which Patti Smith's guitarist, Lenny Kaye, once described as "epiglottal," Leon had a plan. He remembers, laughing, that the singer's voice "was unique, hard to understand, so I figured, well, I'll make it harder to understand. We used a lot of ADT [artificial double tracking] on the record, which is what enhanced another very, very individual

voice: John Lennon's. He used it a lot. Where it sounds like there's two or three of them singing, it's actually one done with tape effects, tape loops. And I remember calling one of the guys at Abbey Road, and putting in a request to George Martin when we were doing the record, trying to figure out how to set it up; it was a bit of a complicated setup for people who hadn't done it before. But it's the same effect that's on all those John Lennon records. So it was used pretty much all over the album. I did a mono mix of the album, which we couldn't use. Which is my favorite thing. And that has less of the ADT on it than the stereo version."

Also interesting on the *Ramones* record is the split of the instruments, hard left and right; when asked about this, Leon laughs again, "Yes, that

ABOVE: Girl groups were a big influence on both the Dictators and the Ramones. The New York Dolls referenced the Shangri-Las directly in their debut studio album—*New York Dolls* (released July 27, 1973)—by quoting a line from the Shangri-Las' 1964 single "Give Him a Great Big Kiss" to open the Dolls' track "Looking for a Kiss."

ABOVE: A 1960 portrait of the Ronettes— Veronica Bennett, Estelle Bennett and Nedra Talley. The Ramones were self-confessed fans of the group, famously covering their 1963 single "Baby, I Love You" on their *End of the Century* album (released February 4, 1980).

was because we couldn't make the mono record. We wanted to make a mono record, but the distributor, ABC at the time, wouldn't put out a mono record, because at that stage everything had to be stereo. So we scrapped the mono mix and tried a conventional stereo mix, which sounded just like a hard-rock band to me. And I said, well, let's do something more. If you really like the Beatles, let's go for the old Beatles three-track recordings, where you'd have almost the whole band on one side, vocals on another side, these three- or four-track recordings that would have like a tambourine on one track, the whole band on another track and vocals on another track, backing vocals on another track. And those records are split very wide stereo as a result of that. With a

kind of tongue-in-cheek homage to the Beatles, I said, okay, I'm gonna do a mix that's hard left and hard right everything."

"Tommy wanted the band to sound streamlined," adds Leon. "He wanted that live sound in the studio, but we wanted to get it more enhanced. So it was not a live recording like a lot of people think. A couple of tracks might have had basic tracks live but there were many guitar overdubs done and the vocals were overdubbed on top of that. But that was pretty much a homage to the '60s rock bands that they liked. They didn't want to head into Midwestern metal and sound like the Stooges and MC5, although I loved that. But it wasn't what they were about—they were a lot more pop and bubble-gum than that."

The resulting album, issued February 4, 1976, is one that set

I LOVE A MAN IN UNIFORM

ABOVE: Roberta Bayley with Debbie Harry in 1980—two women whose early careers were formed alongside the Ramones. Blondie and the Ramones performed regularly together, while Bayley shot the cover photograph for their first album—*Ramones* (released April 23, 1976, pictured **ABOVE, FAR LEFT**). "Oh, they just loved them," says Bayley, asked what Debbie Harry and Chris Stein thought of the Ramones. "I mean, there's no interview that they give about those days that they don't sing the praises of the Ramones. . . . We're all sad that so many people—including all the Ramones—are gone from our group."

The cover of the first Ramones album did as much to burn the concept of the band into pop-culture consciousness as did Arturo's eagle logo or, arguably, even the band's songs, few of which became hits. It's a visual world indeed, and forty years down the line, wearing Ramones' T-shirts supplants, in many youth circles, listening to the Ramones.

"I thought, very much in a weird way," explains Sire's Craig Leon, "that the Ramones were the cultural successors to the Fugs, the band from the '60s whose first album cover was them standing up against a brick wall in the back of one of those alleys, from behind places like CBGB. And then coincidentally—and I don't know whether it's coincidentally or not, you'd have to ask Toni Scott (née Wadler)—but I had mentioned to her that we should do something that's really urban and gritty and New York, that's like this Fugs cover that I showed her."

As it turned out it would be entirely coincidental, with mere fate coughing up a shot just like that. "The Ramones and Sire Records had hired a photographer, as record companies do, to shoot the band," explains eventual photographer of choice, Roberta Bayley. "And they really, really didn't like these pictures, but there wasn't any more budget. All of a sudden, it was, oh my God, we don't have a cover. So Danny Fields called me, 'We have to look at your contact sheets.' They were probably calling Bob Gruen and anybody who had taken their picture. My photo shoot had been in February, so it was down to the wire. I was pretty green as a photographer; I'd bought my camera in November. But they looked at that one contact sheet, and they said, 'We like this picture.' I believe there were three or four rolls of film that I shot on that day. Myself, John Holmstrom, editor of *Punk* magazine, and Legs McNeil just met them at the Ramones' loft. We did some pictures

inside the loft and then we went
downstairs and went two doors down
from Arturo's loft, where there was
a playground, which is now Community
Gardens. Once we got outdoors, we
realized that that was much better
than the shots we'd done in the loft
with the flash because I didn't have
a particularly professional photo
setup running."

"But at this time, the record
company was trying to kind of ease
back the intensity of the Ramones,"
continues Roberta, "so they bought
another picture from that same photo
session, of the Ramones smiling—
as they were throughout the session
in many shots, because we were all
goofing around. We were friends, we
knew each other, the shoot was for
Punk magazine. It wasn't for their
album cover, necessarily."

"So the record company got that one
extra picture, and I think that's the
only official picture of the Ramones
where they're all smiling. They ran it
in some ads. They wanted to take out
a bit of the menacing danger from the
album cover picture. . . . I think a
lot of people—in England, especially—
thought that the Ramones were a gang,
street guys, and maybe they were going
to beat you up, or something. So, yes,
they aren't smiling on the album
cover, but they are smiling in some
of those ads. Literally after that,
Johnny was like, 'We will never smile
again in photos.' In real life, I
believe they were allowed to smile."

the blueprint for punk music at its, by definition, most traditional. *Ramones* struggled to Number 111 on the *Billboard* charts and only became certified gold in 2014—the only Ramones studio album to achieve any RIAA (Recording Industry Association of America) designation. Everybody was talking about it, but nobody bought it, just like the ones that followed: *High Time, Too Much Too Soon*, and *Raw Power*.

Many critics and fans erroneously remember the record as fast. It isn't so much brisk as it is relentless; a churn of cheap electrics consisting of basic, repetitive passages of encapsulated songwriting genius, one after another like some sort of exploding deck of cards. Dee Dee wrote most of the lyrics, with his most notorious being "53rd & 3rd" about his hustling days. A brilliant cover of "Let's Dance" (with the organ playing courtesy of Craig Leon) demonstrated how gleefully old rock 'n' roll fitted into this childish and churlish new format.

However, it's the A-side of the original vinyl that sets the tuneful tone for the band and embodies their goofy worldview. "Blitzkrieg Bop" would become the band's biggest anthem (and future fan favorite at sporting events) and was one of two singles from the album—its original title was the more innocent-sounding "Animal Hop." "Beat on the Brat" and "Judy Is a Punk" are polished pop gems formed from headbanging chord patterns, coupled with lyrics through which Joey caricatures the classic bored punk—stoned on something, but rendered harmless.

The album's second single "I Wanna Be Your Boyfriend" is as good as any girl group-inspired New York Dolls song. "We used tubular bells on that, because they were there in the studio," Leon recalls in our interview. "It was in homage to Phil Spector—they loved the Ronettes' records and so did I. So we had to have bells on something, and they're buried in there with the guitars. . . . Johnny played

ABOVE: Iconic shot of the band walking away from the Supreme Court Building in Washington, DC, taken by Danny Fields in 1976.

INSET: The Ramones' first single, issued by Sire in the United States in February 1976.

ABOVE: Another Roberta Bayley concept that might have conceivably become the cover shot for the first album.

INSET: Ramones' button featuring one of their most famous lines from "Blitzkrieg Bop."

a Mosrite and Doug played a Fender, but there are some guitars that I played on the record on my old '63 Jazzmaster, particularly on 'I Wanna Be Your Boyfriend.'" The track also served as the band's first UK single, which helped reinforce the impact the record would have in the UK, most pertinently on bands quickly converted to the punk ethos.

"I think the Ramones laid down the stylistic parameters for what would go over to England and become a formal style," notes Lenny Kaye during a conversation, "complete with dress and subculture. All the bands had influence over there. Certainly, Blondie had a great deal of success as did us and Television, but we were more punk by attitude. The Ramones really defined what would become the punk rock style when it got over there and got hardened into a very specific type of musical genre."

Other tracks on the album, "Chain Saw" and "I Don't Wanna Go Down to the Basement," play on the band's love for schlock horror movies—later in life

both Johnny and future drummer Marky Ramone would become big '50s movie-poster collectors—and "Now I Wanna Sniff Some Glue" would garner the band some much needed notoriety, leading to a big revolt over the track in the Scottish newspapers, of all places.

"It did give them their biggest headline," recalls *Punk* magazine's John Holmstrom: "'Glue Sniff Disc-Shocker'. But I always figured the Ramones were making drug references in the same way the hippies did, but they were doing it in a joking manner. You know, 'Now I Wanna Sniff Some Glue' is sort of like glue rock instead of acid rock."

"We got a front-page headline in Scotland," Tommy explained in 1977 to *Cheap Thrills*. "Like, the daily newspaper [said] we 'killed twenty kids' in Scotland. They took our cover picture and they cropped it in such a way that it looks like a police lineup. 'These criminals,' you know?" Manager Danny Fields, added "Yeah, over the past year, and our record's only been out there two months, twenty kids died sniffing glue, so they're blaming it on us. I mean, we don't want to see anyone die, but on the other hand, it's kind of fun to be banned because anything that's ever been banned has always done very well."

As for recording the album, not much of a budget was needed because the band was so ready with the songs and none of them were particularly interested in doing too many takes. "I think there was a $10,000 fund," recalls Leon, "but out of that fund they needed to make some money and they needed to make a partial payment for the PA system so they could go and play outside of New York. And I believed they borrowed the rest of the money from Danny Fields, who actually put that PA together, and they didn't even have enough left. But we sat there actually calculating by hand because there weren't any calculators in the office. And we figured out that they could have $6,400 or something out of the $10,000 to make the record. That was all we had, and quite honestly, it was all they needed."

When it came to being in the studio, "they were too quiet," he chuckles. "Too well behaved. They just sat there, and I don't think they ever had any fights about anything, although quite honestly, I don't think they liked each other. Just my personal opinion. They didn't like hanging out, so they'd just play and do their individual things and get going as quickly as possible."

Tommy explained to Ralph Alfonso in 1977: "We're not planning to be a fad. The Ramones are more than songs and stuff—we are an idea, we are a concept. From the album cover down to the lyrics, or down to us, there's meat there. It's not just a front or a façade. We certainly don't intend to be a fad; we intend to entertain people for as long as they want to listen to us. And I think we have a lot to offer them. We're very real. I think we like to be entertaining. We have a sense of humor; I think it's part of rock 'n' roll. Whatever people come to see us for, it's there. It's not an illusion. If somebody thinks, 'Oh, wow, it's really great; it's

rough and tough,' it's there, and if somebody thinks something is amusing, it's amusing."

When it came time for a second record, that balance between amusing and toughness, which Tommy spoke about, was still there. Producer Tony Bongiovi wrought a "heaviness" through his rendering of the band's guitars, which was combined with chord changes that were, arguably, poppier and more sophisticated than on the Ramones' rudimentary debut. Perfectly summing up the record that would become *Leave Home to Gig* magazine back in 1977, Tommy said of Bongiovi, "He's getting us the sounds we want. The new album is going to be heavier and more melodic. The tunes themselves have more of a sing-along quality to them and the heavier songs will have more bite to them."

Lenny Kaye cites a link between the Ramones and the garage bands of the '60s, explaining that this wasn't just pop and '50s rock turned up: "The Ramones took a while to get to their destination. They really tried to turn things back to where it wasn't long guitar solos, with many symphonic sections within a song. They were a reaction against the progressivism of rock and wanted to make it more simple, direct, and catchy. And certainly the garage bands had all that. Their songs were on the surface, seemingly simple, but if you tear them down and looked inside them, there's a lot of interesting hooks and patterns going on. And I think the Ramones were also deceptively simple but there was a precision to their playing—it wasn't kind of aimless jamming. It was very, very structured music. And a lot of the mid-'60s music had that same sense of architecture."

Tony Bongiovi noticed this as well, commenting in an interview for this book: "Tommy had a good ear for pop music. And if you listen to those records, 'Carbona Not Glue,' 'Sheena Is a Punk Rocker,' they're like little, carefully crafted songs that have a different feel, but they all fit within the constraints of what a pop record should sound like. That technique was used to create the punk

"WHEN THE RAMONES HIT ENGLAND, THAT CONVINCED A LOT OF PEOPLE TO PICK UP THE GUITAR AND START PLAYING FOR THE FIRST TIME. HALF THE AUDIENCE—IF NOT MORE THAN THAT—AT THE RAMONES' FIRST SHOW WERE PEOPLE WHO BECAME MUSICIANS IN BANDS. THAT'S WHAT IT USED TO BE LIKE. THE FIRST SHOWS . . . THESE WERE ALL FRIENDS THAT WOULD END UP BEING THE CLASH AND THE ADVERTS."

DAVE VANIAN, THE DAMNED

RIGHT: Rudimentary punk zine *Sniffin' Glue* was as seminal to the scene in the UK as the more polished *Punk* was in New York.

"WHEN THE RAMONES CAME OUT, THEN ALL OF A SUDDEN EVERYBODY WAS GOING 'DO DO DO DO DO DO DO' ON THE BASS. THAT'S WHAT THE RAMONES BROUGHT TO THE MIX: 'DO DO DO DO DO DO.' IT HAD NOTHING TO DO WITH TWO CHORDS OR THREE CHORDS—THAT'S ALL A BUNCH OF BULLSHIT CREATED BY PEOPLE THAT REVIEW ALBUMS AND CALL THEMSELVES ROCK CRITICS. IT NEVER HAD ANYTHING TO DO WITH TWO CHORDS OR THREE CHORDS. I MEAN, THE RAMONES, THEY PROBABLY HAD SOME SONGS THAT HAD TWO CHORDS AND THREE CHORDS, BUT IT WAS JUST A CONVENIENT WAY TO WRITE ABOUT THE MUSIC."

JEFF "MONO MANN" CONOLLY, DMZ

sound, as it became known. You just can't get out there and play random stuff and yell and scream. You've got to have some kind of organization."

"Tommy Erdelyi was my assistant over at Record Plant in New York City . . . right off of Eighth Avenue, when I was recording Jimi Hendrix," continues Bongiovi. "I was like the cleanup engineer, and Tommy was helping me out in the studio. So he recognized the sound that I was getting. I go to work for Media Sound, and Tommy Erdelyi comes over one day, 'I've got a project, and you are the right person for this.' He says, 'I have a band and I want you to co-produce the record with me.' I said, 'Sure, man, how do you want to do this?' He said, 'Well, we're already signed to Warner Bros., Seymour Stein, Sire Records, but you can't listen to this band on a cassette. You have to come and see them.' Now, I normally don't do that until I hear the music, because if there's nothing there, I can't walk out," he laughs. "But out of respect for Tommy, because he's a good guy, I go down to CBGBs, sit right in the front, and out comes Joey Ramone and he had the signature ripped pants and all this, and they start, '1, 2, 3, 4!,' and I don't know if you remember that Maxell commercial with the guy sitting in the chair, and his hair blows back and the lamp falls over? I never heard anything that loud. The sound was so overwhelming."

Suffice it to say, Bongiovi took the gig, and then in October 1976, he applied his magic to making a clean, powerful record where the band's elusive and previously denied sense of heavy metal emerged. Tony and Tommy shared production credit, with engineering credit going to Ed Stasium, who went on to figure prominently in the band's future.

"We went into Sundragon Studios," says Tony, "which was a small studio that was cost-effective, and it was available. They had a Studer 16-track A80, which took about twenty minutes to rewind, and they had a little tiny Trident console in there, which is okay. . . . Whatever we had at Sundragon was good enough for us."

"Here's the problem you have," he explains, when asked about the crafting of the *Leave Home* sound. "When you turn the volume down, you don't have the impact of the live sound or the visual. So if you're making a record, you gotta be able to turn the volume down and still have it sound like a record, okay? We did some things that I don't want to disclose but we also doubled the guitars and we added drums, because it wasn't powerful enough at low volume. We added some instruments because I needed texture to be able to reinforce what they did. And these subtleties are all about playing it at a low volume, okay? So we doubled the guitars, the drums, we doubled the voice, we recorded Joey with an SM57. Nobody does that. It's a crappy microphone to use for voice. It's a cardioid dynamic microphone, and usually we use a condenser microphone to record somebody's voice."

"When it came time to mix it, it wouldn't mix," Bongiovi adds, who found a way to capitalize on the situation. "So I'm sitting in the studio, saying, how the hell do I get this to sound right? I put so much high frequency on the tape when I mixed it, it would hurt your ears. So I called Bob Ludwig over at Masterdisk, and I said, 'I'm sending you down the tape, but you have to undo what I did. Because when you do that, it'll sound right.' In order for me to get the pieces to come together, I had to equalize the sound a certain way. That's the first time that I ever made a record and then depended on the mastering facility to work in conjunction and coordination with what I was doing."

The Ramones' *Leave Home* album (meaning exactly that—taking their show on the road) hit the streets on January 10, 1977, and instantly upon playing "Glad to See You Go" and "Gimme, Gimme Shock Treatment," the listener is hit with a blast of roiling guitars and drums that somehow sound as though the music has been filtered through rose-colored glasses and glazed with gleeful pop melody. The effect is strengthened by Joey

PUNK ROCK

Punk magazine—cooked up by John Holmstrom, Eddie "Legs" McNeil, and Ged Dunn Jr., three buddies from Connecticut—only lasted eighteen issues. But the pioneering rag, with its cartoony hand-drawn text, its action sequence photography, and its hopelessly urban sense of humor, did much to define this new thing called punk rock. And by extension, the magazine's pick for best and most discussed example of a band making this new music—*Punk*'s new content clowns—would be the Ramones.

"Oh, we were terribly important," begins Holmstrom, asked about the influence the magazine had, simply through the name of it. "It was a very obscure word, only known to the readers of rags like *Creem* magazine. We introduced it into the mainstream. I think because the magazine was named *Punk*, and it was a new music scene, people were interested and we were the most obvious publication covering it in New York. It didn't all begin here but the important scene was here."

"So every once in a while *Creem* would mention punk rock," continues John, offering more on the etymology. "The most obvious one is when Alice Cooper was voted Punk of the Year in 1974. In September '75, before we published *Punk* magazine, the *Aquarian* out of New Jersey did a cover story on punk rock at CBGB. For the cover, they chose this weird-looking guy with whiskers and a floppy hat and huge bellbottoms, so nobody had put a visual element to punk yet. You know, in late '75, punk was going to be Bruce Springsteen and Patti Smith. They were getting all the hype. And to me, punk rock was more about fast, hard, and loud. To me, the Dictators and the Ramones were the Beatles and the Rolling Stones of punk rock. They were the two bands that inspired me to start *Punk* magazine. Originally it was going to be a more generic title, but Ged and Legs insisted on calling it *Punk*. And I knew it would get us some attention, but I didn't realize how much it would limit our ability to write about anything else."

Adds *Punk* photographer Roberta Bayley, "They had the idea for the magazine largely based on their work with the Dictators. That album [*Go Girl Crazy!*, released March 1975] was already out, and the whole thing—cars, girls, sex, and beer—was like their teenage idea of what they were trying to do in the magazine. But then when they saw the Ramones, it was like the living embodiment of their whole thing. So they became huge, huge Ramones fans, and put them in right away. And then by the third issue, they were going to be on the cover."

John's treatment of the Ramones within the pages of *Punk*—the anarchic journalistic tone, yes, but more so his comic and cartoon visual presentation—would become ingrained in the band's aesthetic, underscored by John's extended hand into the graphics of *Rocket to Russia* and most paramount, the cover of *Road to Ruin*.

"Well, from the first issue of *Punk*, we did a big centerfold poster of them," recalls John. "And the photos weren't intentionally taken to look as very stark, black-and-white, and vivid as they came out. They did a great job, really capturing the visual image of the Ramones. Of course, the first record cover of the Ramones came from a photo shoot we did. Johnny was always asking me, 'What do you think of this?' 'What do you think of that?' and we definitely influenced each other. Joey did a lot of work for the magazine. He came up with the idea for Punk of the Month and did some crude illustrations for our

BELOW: John Holmstrom and occasional *Punk* magazine employee Joey Ramone.

OPPOSITE BOTTOM: Famous "out of his element" shot of Joey from "Mutant Monster Beach Party"—a special *fumetti* photographic edition of *Punk* drawn and directed by John Holmstrom and photographed by Roberta Bayley in July/August 1976.

Punk's original run was fifteen issues from early 1976 through to 1979, but the innovation and enthusiasm that went into its making ensured the legendary status it enjoys today.

Iggy Pop interview, which was done at the Ramones' loft."

"When we interviewed them for the third issue, we said we'd put them on the cover if they got a record deal. And sure enough, they got the record deal, shortly after. I debate this with Mickey [Joey's brother] all the time, because the timing is a little off, but from what Danny [Fields] told us . . . the first part of the magazine

to get printed was that centerfold. And Danny heard that we had the centerfold printed and he wanted to see it right away, so Legs brought a bunch over to him at some party. Danny later told us that that was the straw that broke the camel's back and convinced Seymour Stein to sign them."

"*Punk* wasn't really a fanzine, but it was a magazine written by fans of the music," reflects Roberta, in closing. "There wasn't any way that *Punk* was going to be told we've got to put Rick Derringer on the cover because their company is going to buy an ad. Their choices in *Punk* were very much made by John Holmstrom and what their tastes were, rather than what's going to be big. But of course we all thought the Ramones and Debbie Harry were going to be big, and that Television was going to be playing Madison Square Garden. We all thought the Ramones should've been at the top of the charts and the biggest thing since sliced bread. But sometimes not having that happen, your influence just continues and continues, which is what's happened with them."

Ramone's compositions "I Remember You" and "Oh, Oh I Love Her So," which seem to embrace, even more studiously, the band's '60s sensibilities.

"There was a lot of the Brill-building romanticism in what Joey did," recalls Lenny Kaye during our interview. "And I think that's what sets the Ramones apart from many who would follow them, is that they had a sense of heart on their sleeve, and it made their music not as confrontational as is usually thought. It had a certain open arms to it. You know, total romance, total longing and yearning. And certainly Joey, who was one part misfit, drew upon that sense of romantic idealism, especially as the Ramones got deeper into their own complexity. They might've started as chants set to music, but really, by the time they moved into their middle chronology, they were definitely exploring more tender ways in which to express emotion. As for Joey's voice,

it came from somewhere in the back of his throat. It was a sweet voice and certainly unusual and not your classic rocker's voice. It had a lot of Ronnie Spector in it, that kind of bouncing vibrato, a very wide vibrato and kind of expressive. It definitely came from a strange place in his larynx."

The single "Carbona Not Glue" has a similar Beach Boys feel, although the lyrics are a humorously contentious follow-up to the band's early glue song. "Glue wasn't exactly the Cadillac of drugs," quipped Dee Dee to *Spin* magazine in 2001. "It wasn't so much a drug as it was a *substitute* for drugs." However, those in charge at the English label, remembering the Scotland flap, balked and switched out the track for "Babysitter." In the end, Sire in the United States conceded as well after about 5,000 copies had been released.

"Suzy Is a Headbanger" is more of the same and is also a sequel, of sorts, to "Judy Is a Punk." "Pinhead"

BELOW: The Ramones with a fan and his poster, May 19, 1977, Liverpool, UK.

makes use of Tony's guitar crunch for evil instead of good, seeing the band putting aside the sunshine chords and cranking out a heavy metal classic. Is "Pinhead" an example of the band at its purposefully dimmest? "Someone wrote that we're dumb," said Johnny to *Punk* in 1976, putting a twist on the idea. "We can't play. I hate to read that we're dumb. There's a lot of dumb groups. . . . We don't want to get into a big heavy intellectual thing. We just want to play rock 'n' roll. Just being original is showing intelligence, I think."

"Zippy the Pinhead, right?" explains John Holmstrom in our conversation. "That and 'Pinhead' were both inspired by the release of Tod Browning's *Freaks*. I mean, everybody went to see *Freaks*, which had been banned since the '30s, because it showed real circus freaks. Tod Browning was famous. He directed a lot of very infamous horror movies, and regular movies. He was one of the great silent film directors. Then he wanted to make this movie *Freaks*, and it kind of ended his career. It was banned, because it was too sick. It came out around the time they enforced the Hayes code on films. And that's where the Ramones got the lyric, 'Gabba Gabba Hey.' In the film, *Freaks*, they [make a gobbling noise.] And it inspired the Zippy the Pinhead cartoon character, which is why Johnny wanted the pinhead on the missile on the back of *Rocket to Russia*."

Other *Leave Home* highlights include "Commando," one of the band's most lethal heavy metal rockers, certainly until the mid-'80s, as well as happy cover "California Sun." "The covers were good ideas," muses Tony Bongiovi. "They were good songs that worked then, and they worked in their style. So we did it because, hey, there's a cool song, let's cover that one. It wasn't, oh, we can't write, so we've got to cover—no. That just happened to work. Just like Brian Wilson would cover songs with the Beach Boys." When asked if he had been aware that the other New York "punk" band, the Dictators, had already covered "California Sun" on their 1975 album *Go Girl Crazy!*, Tony says, laughing, "No, I didn't know there was another version of that out there.

DWAIN ESPER PRESENTS

FREAKS

LOUELLA PARSONS *SAYS—*
FOR PURE SENSATIONALISM "FREAKS" TOPS ANY PICTURE
YET PRODUCED. IT'S MORE FANTASTIC AND GROTESQUE
THAN ANY SHOCKER EVER WRITTEN.

EXCLUSIVE FOREIGN DISTRIBUTION CONTROLLED BY
EXCELSIOR PICT. CORP.
NEW YORK 19, U.S.A.

Probably if I did, I wouldn't have done mine. But here's the good part—we hit with ours."

The record closes with a mid-level rocker called "You Should Never Have Opened That Door," another horror movie-inspired song added to the canon. "That's a song which might have gone on the last album," Johnny later remarked in an interview with *Gig* magazine in 1977. "It's about this guy who gouges out people's eyes and sticks them in his blind daughter's sockets. The cellar's full of eyeless people bumping into each other." Joey added, "My eyes have been hurting me since I saw it."

In essence, *Leave Home* represents a sharp focusing of the Ramones' concept, which had been tentative and up for grabs on their debut; by their second time around, it was all about churning guitars propelled by simple

drums—albeit drums appointed with a sly percussive ear candy, which despite being barely audible, gave them their distinctive sound.

"Johnny cut out all the inessentials," reflects Lenny Kaye during our conversation. "Any solos that came through were minimal to the max. He really took rhythm guitar to its most jackhammer. That's kind of an innovation that is not as well regarded as somebody who plays thirty-two or sixty-four notes to the bar. He really cut out all the underbrush. He reduced the guitar to its most elemental, and in doing that, he created a music that was as precise, pointed, strong, and accurate as a sharpshooter."

There would be more press attention for the band's second album than there had been for their debut—most of it was favorable, but alas, the record

ABOVE: The original cut of Tod Browning's *Freaks*, issued February 20, 1932, ran ninety minutes. Only the edited version, at sixty-four minutes, remains, with the removed footage considered to be lost.

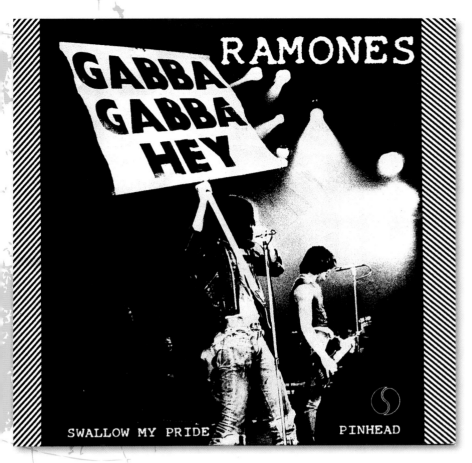

RAMONES

GABBA GABBA HEY

SWALLOW MY PRIDE   PINHEAD

still stalled at a lowly Number 148 on the US *Billboard* chart. The semi-ballad "I Remember You" was launched as a single, but failed to chart, while the similarly saccharin "Swallow My Pride" fared slightly better, reaching Number 36 on the UK chart.

The journalist Caroline Coon commented on the album's release in the UK music magazine *Melody Maker*: "The Ramones' first album was so good, whatever followed was bound to be dissected under a microscope of hyper-criticism. Our New York heroes have achieved the impossible, however. They've roped in the bold Tony Bongiovi to polish up the production but they've managed to retain the raw, spark-spewing, chain-saw grind of their original sound. On record, these boys are rough. In the flesh, they're reassuringly gentle. Joey Ramone . . . is so shy that a two-second glance is likely to knock him over. He makes up for this diffidence by singing like an air-stabbing flick knife."

In 1976, the Ramones left the East Coast and toured much of America, also playing Toronto twice and more significantly, twice in the UK. In Britain, they further ignited the emerging punk scene—amplifying the electrifying effect of their first

record with a packed house of two thousand catching their July 4 show at the Roundhouse in Camden, London. Los Angeles was another tour highlight, with the band, who were permanently scrapping with each other at this point, making their way out there in a van and finding themselves significantly inspired by the unexpected response on the other side of the country.

In 1977, the Ramones mounted a full American campaign, along with a European tour and a blanketing of the UK, with gigs taking them from Glasgow, Scotland to the other end of the country in Penzance, Cornwall. By now, the band had planted themselves into pop-culture consciousness worldwide. However tiny the seed might have been, the Ramones were a recognized and loved cartoon of a band; their devotees might have been few, but those few were intense in their devotion.

The pressure was on for the Ramones to capitalize on their position as the critics' darling band that they'd always been, and to do something—anything—about their lack of ability to sell records.

"Nothing!" laughs Tony Bongiovi, when asked what was done differently on the sessions for what would become *Rocket to Russia*, the album cited most as the band's best record. "Whatever worked on that first one, I did the same thing on the second one, because if it wasn't broke, why should I fix it? The songs were different, obviously; newer songs and they were more mature as a band, so the playing was a little bit different. But there was no reason for me to change anything and as a result those two records sound similar in a lot of ways. We used the same drums, same guitars, same amplifiers. We didn't go out and buy Marshall™ amplifiers or a new set of Yamahas™. Ramones were a brute force. That's what they did. You know, you don't want to change it. By the time I got them, they were rehearsed. Okay, start the tape, let's go. Both records could run sequentially and it would've worked."

Rocket to Russia would see its birthing delayed from the summer of '77 to November 4 of that year.

"Again everything was recorded at Sundragon," notes Bongiovi, working with a budget this time upwards of $25,000. "It was mixed at Media, but by then I had Power Station, and I did some of the mixing there as well." Although the team of Tony and Tommy was intact, again, Ed Stasium is often cited as secret weapon, doing much of the heavy lifting on a record, which, if anything, carries itself with a little more authority than *Leave Home*. The product mix is near identical—trace elements of metal occurring within "Teenage Lobotomy" and "We're a Happy Family." "Rockaway Beach," "Cretin Hop," and "Sheena Is a Punk Rocker" were happy punk—anthemic, and with hit potential—these songs and the aforementioned heavier tracks, were all sequels of sorts; echoes from the previous two records.

"Heavier and louder and faster," is how Joey characterized the record for *Hit Parader* in 1978. "They don't all sound like they were written by one person; they're diversified. We write all the songs as singles, as being number one hits, you know?" added Dee Dee. "Everybody just works together writing the songs. I know it may be hard to believe, but it's the truth. Someone will come up with an idea and the other three will elaborate on it or else we'll actually sit down and say, let's write a song and just invent one."

At the more balladic end of the scale, there is "I Wanna Be Well," which would have been a title track of sorts if the band had called the album *Get Well*, as they'd originally debated doing. "Locket Love" is also in this wheelhouse, its briskness countered by the softness of the guitar tracks and the surf-rock backing vocals. "I Can't Give You Anything" proposes a Ramones twist on Buddy Holly and Eddie Cochran. There were also two covers this time: "Do You Wanna Dance?"—keeping it light and sympathetic—and "Surfin' Bird," indicative of the Ramones' systematic ability to Frankenstein an old chestnut into a punk pogo. "Here Today, Gone Tomorrow" is the record's purest ballad and one of its gems, while "I Don't Care" finds the band finally putting on record one of their earliest written and starkest songs lyrically.

"There was not a lot of artifice involved in the Ramones," reflects John Holmstrom. "There was an honesty in their lyrics and that's why it worked. A lot of creative people have trouble being brutally honest about life, about their lives and about their thoughts and feelings. And I think that's one of the reasons why the Ramones are interesting. There is something that's relatable on a human level in many of their songs. A song like 'I Don't Care' I think is so brilliant . . . obviously he cares, you know? Joey says a lot in a few words, without saying practically anything."

Holmstrom was tasked with the cartooning of *Rocket to Russia*'s back cover, as well as its inner sleeve. The front cover featured a shot taken

ABOVE: If there was any doubt that the Ramones were darlings of the press . . . see above ad for their first two albums in *Rolling Stone*, March 10, 1977.

OPPOSITE: An interesting bill for the July 4, 1976, show in London, with each of these three bands celebrating nascent rock 'n' roll culture in its own complex manner.

ROUNDHOUSE CHALK FARM N.W.1
SUNDAY 4th JULY at 5·30 p.m

STRAIGHT MUSIC PRESENTS

FLAMIN' GROOVIES
RAMONES
THE STRANGLERS

ANDY DUNKLEY 'THE LIVIN' JUKE BOX'

ADM. £1·60 (inc vat) IN ADVANCE R HOUSE BOX OFF. 267-2564
or LONDON THEATRE BOOKINGS shaft.av.w1. 439-3371 or AT DOOR

"AS SOON AS THE RAMONES WENT AND PLANTED THE FLAG, IT WAS LIKE, I CAN DO THIS. BECAUSE THEY MADE IT SEEM EASY—ALTHOUGH REALLY IT WASN'T. BECAUSE TO PLAY LIKE THEM IS NOT THAT EASY. BUT THEY HAD SIMPLIFIED THE WHOLE COMPLEXITY OF IT, TO THIS ONE EFFORTLESS THING. AND THE BRITS WERE ESPECIALLY TAKEN BY IT, BECAUSE THE BRITS LOVE A UNIFORM AND THEY LOVE TO BE PART OF A GANG. SO THIS WAS READY-MADE WITH LEATHER JACKETS, EVERYTHING, WITH THE ORIGINS BEING SOMEWHAT FROM THE CHRISTOPHER STREET GAY UNDERGROUND."
RALPH ALFONSO, *CHEAP THRILLS* MAGAZINE AND THE CRASH 'N' BURN CLUB, TORONTO

BELOW: "I saw them live first," says Lenny Kaye, asked about the Ramones on stage, pictured here in Liverpool, 1977. "They were such a great concept and an idea, in the sense that they were kind of like a package, and they were fun. They had a very unique take on reducing the music to its building blocks, essentially. The spirit of rock 'n' roll had been getting lost, and so it was time to return to the core values, what I like to call the original sin of rock 'n' roll."

by manager Danny Fields, designed to evoke the magic of the debut record's cover image—nobody had liked the artier image used on *Leave Home*.

"Johnny was really happy with it," explains John, who really added to the band's image as cartoon characters. "He said, I figure first things our fans are going to do when they pick up the record is smoke a joint, drink a beer, put on the record, and then look at the cover. And that's what record covers were like then—they were like music videos. But it backfired a bit, because the Ramones were not taken seriously as musicians. They were written off as a joke by certain people."

"But it was all their ideas," Holmstrom continues. "The inside sleeve came first. Johnny wanted all the song lyrics illustrated. Because I hadn't heard the songs, all I had to go by was the lyrics. As well, we did a photo shoot with Joey, at the Ramones loft. He wanted to do 'Teenage Lobotomy' as a dinner layout. So we bought a cow brain and put it on a plate, with as fancy dinnerware as we could get. And then after we finished, we're having a few beers, and we decided to go to CBGB and kind of play with the brain. So we put the brain on the bar and on the stage or whatever. And that's the night we found out that Elvis died, so you can put a date to that. But I'd brought all these different ideas to Johnny, who said he needed them all in two days. It was a lot of work, but it's also how I got the money to get moved into my apartment. I was getting evicted, and I've been here ever since. Johnny liked the inside sleeve so much, he said, 'I'd like you to do the back cover,' to which I thought, cool, amazing.

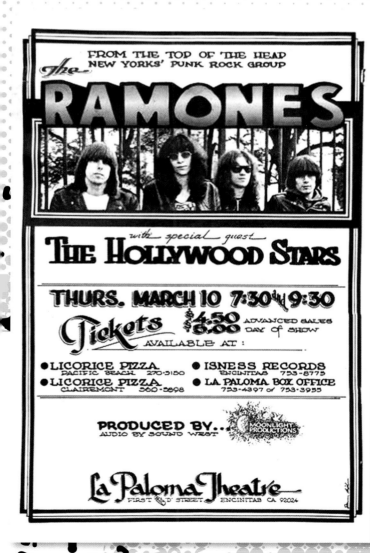

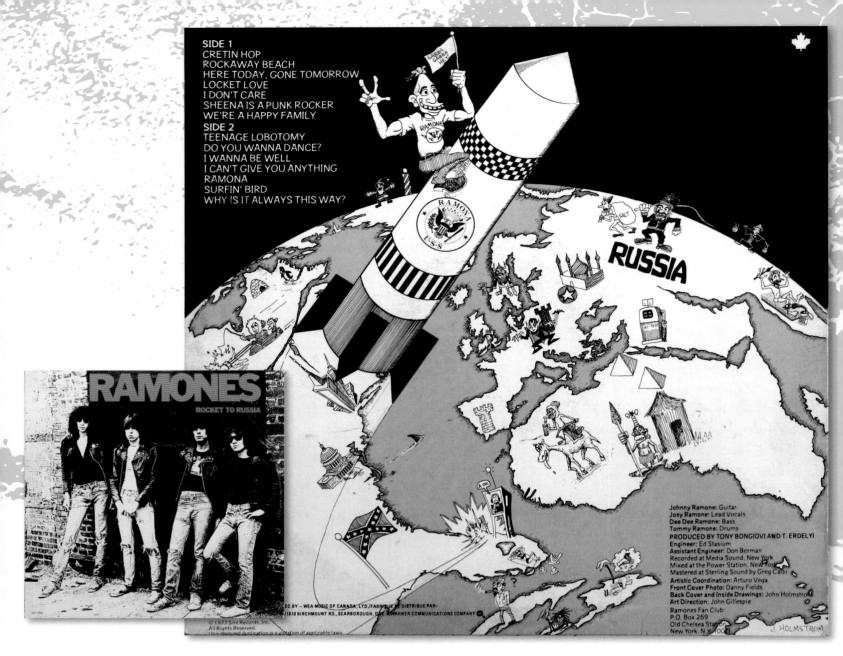

SIDE 1
CRETIN HOP
ROCKAWAY BEACH
HERE TODAY, GONE TOMORROW
LOCKET LOVE
I DON'T CARE
SHEENA IS A PUNK ROCKER
WE'RE A HAPPY FAMILY
SIDE 2
TEENAGE LOBOTOMY
DO YOU WANNA DANCE?
I WANNA BE WELL
I CAN'T GIVE YOU ANYTHING
RAMONA
SURFIN' BIRD
WHY IS IT ALWAYS THIS WAY?

RUSSIA

RAMONES
ROCKET TO RUSSIA

Johnny Ramone: Guitar
Joey Ramone: Lead Vocals
Dee Dee Ramone: Bass
Tommy Ramone: Drums
PRODUCED BY TONY BONGIOVI AND T. ERDELYI
Engineer: Ed Stasium
Assistant Engineer: Don Berman
Recorded at Media Sound, New York
Mixed at the Power Station, New York
Mastered at Sterling Sound by Greg Calbi
Artistic Coordination: Arturo Vega
Front Cover Photo: Danny Fields
Back Cover and Inside Drawings: John Holmstrom
Art Direction: John Gillespie
Ramones Fan Club:
P.O. Box 269
Old Chelsea Station
New York, N.Y. 10011

And he described what he wanted; he described the missile, the different characters, the globe—it was all in his head."

Despite releasing three singles from the record, *Rocket to Russia* peaked at Number 49 on the *Billboard* chart, with the band complaining that archrivals the Sex Pistols had given punk a bad name with their downright nihilism and their cranky disposition on stage, and that their onstage antics had begun to rile up crowds at live shows. Whatever the cause, it soon became customary for the audience to gleefully hurl verbal abuse, spit, and whatever else they could throw at the stage during punk concerts.

It was all too much for Tommy, who would be off the drum stool and producing only when it came to the band's next album, *Road to Ruin*.

Tony Bongiovi recalls, "I went to see them live at the Academy of Music, and I'm standing backstage, and they're getting ready to go out and I saw the audience throwing things on the stage. And I said to Tommy when it was done, I've never seen a band where people throw stuff because they love you. But he wanted to get more involved in film, and when I had Power Station, he used to come over there. . . . I said, 'Listen, I've got to go see my cousin Jon, play. You want to take a ride with me to the Meadowbrook in New Jersey?' So we went out there to look at Jon, and on the way back, I said, 'Do you want to work on this with me?' And he said, 'No, I don't really hear anything there.' So that was Jon Bon Jovi, okay? And I ended up doing that by myself. No, Tommy wanted to get into film and he was a highly

ABOVE AND INSET: The *Rocket to Russia* (released November 4, 1977) album artwork saw the classic Ramones stance on the front juxtaposed with the creative energy of John Holmstrom's cartoons on the back.

"I THOUGHT WE WERE PRETTY PUNK, ACTUALLY. WE FIT RIGHT IN WITH ALL THE PUNKS BECAUSE OF OUR AGE AND OUR ATTITUDE, EVEN OUR MUSIC—WE WERE PUNKS. THE FIRST TOUR WE EVER DID WITH THE RUNAWAYS WAS THREE MONTHS ON THE ROAD WITH THE RAMONES. THAT WAS PRETTY COOL. . . . AND THE RAMONES WOULD GET HANDFULS OF STUFF THROWN AT THEM ON STAGE, AND SO THEY USED TO PUT CHICKEN WIRE UP AT THE FRONT OF THE STAGE, TO PROTECT THE BAND."

LITA FORD, THE RUNAWAYS

ABOVE: Sleeves for the 1977 singles from *Rocket to Russia*.
FAR LEFT: "Rockaway Beach," the Belgian 12-inch edition including two additional tracks— "Teenage Lobotomy" and "Beat On the Brat" (the latter from the *Ramones* album).
CENTER: "Rockaway Beach," 7-inch released in Germany by Philips with "Locket to Love" on the B-side.
FAR RIGHT: "Sheena Is a Punk Rocker," the French 7-inch again under the Philips label with "Commando" on the B-side.

intelligent person. And he understood the inner workings of how the record business worked, and he wanted to do other things than go out and play on stage. I think the main reason is he didn't want to go out and play live anymore. The drumming is not as creative as it is hard-driving, so it could be boring. But he was always concerned he'd get hit in the head with something. But Tommy had been in charge. You could say he was the manager of the band in the beginning. It was all his idea. All of it was. And those are the people that he brought together to be able to express his idea musically."

Also, by all accounts, being in the Ramones was driving Tommy nuts. "He's got multiple personalities, depending on what mood he's in," said Tommy later of "drill-sergeant" Johnny. "Basically

he had his ideas of what the group should be, okay? But as far as I know, he didn't hold the band hostage on anything . . . if they followed his advice, it was because they wanted to, all right? But he had his say. He had his ideas, which wasn't necessarily the idea of every person in the band. He could be a very genuinely nice guy, and kind of generous, and other times he could be different. So it depends what mood you'd catch him in actually."

Reflecting on his own neuroses, Tommy explained: "That was caused by the band. They did it to me. Ha! If you're cooped up in a van with the Ramones, it can eventually get to you. I was fairly normal before I got into the band! I don't recommend joining that ship for too long a period. They themselves were more or less comfortable. It's just that my way of thinking and their way of thinking . . . trying to figure it out, reality was slowly slipping away. That's what the Ramones will do to you, you know what I mean? Their world, what happens is it's like when a person joins some kind of cult. There's constant brainwashing going on of sorts. Which means, either somebody leaves the cult or stays and loves it. There's a way of thinking or indoctrination, and one either takes to it and becomes part of the cult or says, 'I'd rather have my own way of thinking, you know? Thank you.' So it's a groupthink type of thing that can just be very restrictive."

In discussing *Rocket to Russia*, Lenny Kaye notes that, "The Ramones expanded on their vision, but of course, the songs I remember are from when they became the standard-bearer for punk rock. The songs are catchy—"Sheena Is a Punk Rocker," "Rockaway Beach"—this is them at their most pure. They would figure out a little more about how to break into the hearts and minds of the mainstream music business as they went along, but to me, I liked them when they were more unformed, and trying to get control of the whipsaw of their music, and trying to get the strength and energy together to sustain this for more than twenty—twenty-five minutes."

"This is the one that is supposed to put them over the top," wrote *Twisted*'s Kathy Hammonds on the release of the album. "Their record company think so, so they've got ads in every rag from the *Aryan Pig Weekly* to the *National Enquirer*. The press think so; their coverage has been relentless. I think so, and the record buying public? Well (fanfare, please) *Rocket to Russia* has made the top 50 on the *Billboard* charts. Top 40 stuff if I've ever heard it. Pop enough for AM and palatable enough for FM."

By degrees more vociferous in his support was *Stage Life*'s John Lamont, who argued that, "*Rocket to Russia* offers encouragement to the belief that the punk idiom has as much to offer as established approaches to rock, and more. The jerk-offs who call this nihilistic are paranoid beyond recognition. Ramones are making statements on the issues of insanity and death, without indulging in a lot of rancid emotionalism. Their work has affirmative power without burying its head in some romantic sand dune. The very fact that it frightens blue-nosed idiots and those they mislead stands as positive proof that this stuff is on target."

OPPOSITE: A chaotic, punk-in-spirit ad from the UK's *New Music Express* on April 22, 1978; the Ramones got moderate support from Sire in the influential UK music weeklies, which were experiencing great power in England in the '70s.

PAGES 62–63: The band in their element, and the crowd too! The Ramones clearly rocking Eric's in Liverpool, UK on May 19, 1977.

03

1978-
1979

ROAD TO RUIN AND
THE END OF PUNK

ROAD TO RUIN AND THE END OF PUNK

By 1978, scribes across the pond in the UK had declared punk long dead—it was even quipped that punk died when the Clash signed to CBS Records—while America had barely rallied its forces to join the revolution. Yet it was in the States that punk evolved into hardcore—in the Ramones' own backyard, as well as in southern California. Still, by the time the Ramones created their more thoughtful 1978 *Road to Ruin* album, punk had become post-punk in the UK, and in America something we might call "new wave" was born—basically a more radio-friendly take on punk,

represented by the Cars, the Knack, the Romantics, and even Tom Petty.

In essence, new wave in America proved through its stylistic range that the journalistic pigeon-holing of this diverse music failed to acknowledge the intellectual heft of punk as a movement.

As far as New York was concerned, punk was a philosophy and not precisely what the Dead Boys put on their *Young Loud and Snotty* record. The Ramones would never play the snarling punk game, and as the so-called end of punk loomed, it was prescient of them to work even harder on arrangement and range.

PAGE 64: The band as seen in the 1980s with the new addition of Marky.

OPPOSITE: Cleveland's Dead Boys, pictured here at CBGB on April 29, 1977, were perhaps the punkiest, heaviest, most clichéd of the bigger US punk bands, or more accurately, most similar to the popular conception of what a punk band from the UK was like.

THE
SOUND
OF
THE

A NEW WORLD

SeX PisTOLs
punk?
The Clash
Jam
Generation X
Rocker
New wave
RIOT

Stranglers in full throttle
"SOME of the greatest songs that have ever been written have only got three chords," say the Stranglers in their defence. "You're inco...
if you a...

DAMNED HOT!
PAGE 33

NO CYCLING ALLOWED

RAT SCABIES playing guitar, not necessarily in Paris. Pic: CARLOS

With *Rocket to Russia* failing to trouble the charts and punk being declared dead—or at least sick, twisted, and worthy of scorn—the Ramones soldiered on without improvement to their commercial prospects, although this time Tommy and wise engineer Ed Stasium took the reigns of the production.

On *Road to Ruin* the band were steadfast in representing the definition of punk that applied only to them, not the one that had gotten away from them and was being propagated by the Dead Boys (for some, a mutation of the Ramones), not to mention British archrivals the

Sex Pistols and to a certain extent the Damned and the Adverts.

"They hated it," says John Holmstrom, when asked what the band thought of being called punks. "Most of the bands avoided the label. They never admitted to being a punk band. They always called themselves a rock 'n' roll band. Nobody wanted to be part of the next fad. They'd just seen folk rock and acid rock and prog rock and glam, all these different things, and they didn't want to be part of a fad and have a four-year shelf life. But by 1982, Johnny was giving interviews where he said, 'We're a

ABOVE: Contentious theory: Punk might have been invented in the US but the UK quickly took over and perfected it. The Sex Pistols used their cover art and T-shirts to shout even louder about their own brand of anarchy. This unused Sex Pistols artwork created by Brian Cooke in 1977 is a snapshot of the hedonistic London punk scene.

ABOVE: Dee Dee takes a punch or two from the crowd at one of their first gigs in Holland in 1977.

punk rock band.' By then they realized they were not going to get huge by being mainstream. We didn't know what punk was going to become when we started it. I thought it was going to become bigger and more popular in the US, the way it was everywhere else in the world but America. They couldn't wait to shovel dirt on the grave in England—that's what they delight in. And the ironic thing is that punk rock never ended. It just started getting bigger and bigger and bigger. And it was the opposite of a fad."

However, many would feel that Holmstrom is going out on a limb with this supposition. Yes, punk did rise up into the '90s, and there would be omnipresent hardcore on both sides of the pond through the '80s. But in many ways punk did indeed die by 1978, or more accurately, it failed to lift off, lacking even a single commercial hit act in 1976 or 1977, and none after that— except for bands who essentially had to leave the fray to be noticed at all.

Into this stagnant environment waded the Ramones, tweaking the music to offer a little more ear candy, and touring much the same way as they had for the first three records. The biggest change was that they had hired

a new drummer in Marc "Marky Ramone" Bell, previously of hippie hard rockers Dust, but more in tune with his other former bandmembers—Richard Hell and the Voidoids, also in the Sire stable.

Marky, in interview with the author, comments on the burgeoning UK punk scene: "Malcolm McLaren took his style to England and put it on the Sex Pistols. Told Johnny Rotten and all those guys to cut their hair, put holes in their clothes, and then the Sex Pistols were formed. Malcolm wanted Richard Hell to be their lead singer, and then they got Johnny Lydon, cleaned him up, dyed his hair, and they became the Spice Girls of punk rock. And they had one good album and that was it.

Our record [*Blank Generation*] was out in '77, and we toured with the Clash in England for five weeks, in the fall of '77, when the original punk thing was really at its height. Richard was a great writer, but very self-indulgent in the drug problem, which was unfortunate. . . . It was

his necessity to always go cop what he had to cop. I wanted to play. I felt that the band was deteriorating, and when we came back from the Clash tour, he didn't want to tour anymore and I did. And that's when Tommy Ramone left the Ramones and went to produce, and that's when I joined the Ramones. I was always friends with them, and they knew of my drumming, and they asked me to join up. Because I wanted to play. I wanted to continue to record—Richard didn't."

"For the second and third album, a lot of the songs were co-written by everybody," Tommy recalled in an interview with Mark Prindle in 2003. "The *Road to Ruin* album, I contributed a lot to what you can hear through all the arrangements. I helped them work together the arrangements. A lot of the stuff that you hear on that record that sounds a little, let's say 'progressive;' that's pretty much me."

So, Tommy was back in the fold for the recording, until Johnny told him that he wasn't going to receive any of the publishing monies on the record.

ABOVE: Richard Hell & the Voidoids in 1977, left to right: Robert Quine (guitar), Richard Hell (bass and lead vocals), Ivan Julian (guitar) and future Ramone, Marc "Marky Ramone" Bell (drums).

"THE RAMONES WERE REALLY GOOD. WE FIRST SAW THEM IN YOUNGSTOWN, OHIO. THIS WAS WHEN THE FIRST ALBUM CAME OUT AND IT WAS ONE OF THEIR FIRST GIGS OUTSIDE OF NEW YORK, I THINK. AND WE JUST HIT IT OFF WITH THEM. . . . AT CBGB, JOEY GOT US PAST THE TRIAL. WE WOULD'VE HAD TO HAVE GONE AND PLAYED AN AUDITION NIGHT. JOEY WENT UP TO HILLY KRISTAL AND FIBBED AND SAID HE'D SEEN US AND THAT WE WERE REALLY GOOD, AND HE HADN'T. AND HE BYPASSED IT AND GOT US A REGULAR SLOT."

CHEETAH CHROME, DEAD BOYS

Tommy later commented: "Well, I think he was pressured by the others. I don't know. I can just guess that that was what happened. I think they were under the illusion that I was gonna be getting a lot of money or something. I don't think they entirely understood how. I don't know. It didn't really make sense actually. I assume that they probably resented me leaving the band. I think there might have been some greed involved too. I never really asked them the question why. I didn't put up a big deal, you know."

Many critics and Ramones-watchers have framed their fourth album as showcasing a pronounced pop tilt to the band; however a closer look at the tracks doesn't quite back this up. "They started on the *Road to Ruin* album," Tommy remembered. "Basically, here we were making all these great albums that weren't going anywhere. And I thought from the second album on, especially *Rocket to Russia*, that they'd be a natural fit . . . that nationally the albums would be accepted. Certainly *Rocket to Russia*.

So I guess they figured that they had to turn into some kind of a commercial band. They were always going for something that would give them a hit or whatever, so they were on that road and they pretty much stayed on that road on and off for the rest of their career. But they never lost their songwriting talent, and some of those records are really good. Especially the records near the end. It's amazing that a group that had been together for that long under such trying circumstances and so much pressure could put out records that still sound good and generate good reviews and everything. They sound great."

Recorded in May and through June 1978 at Media Sound, *Road to Ruin* was released on September 21, 1978, with the first two singles being provocatively radio-friendly. "'Don't Come Close' was the first single," explains John Holmstrom in our discussion. "They were going for it, for a commercial breakthrough.

(continued on page 76)

THE FIFTH RAMONE

ARTURO VEGA AND THE RAMONES' AESTHETIC

"Fifth Ramone" Arturo Vega, who passed on at the age of sixty-five in 2013, will forever be famous for his designing of the Ramones' "presidential seal" logo—governmental, but extra cheeky through the inclusion of a bat, in homage to "Beat on the Brat." However, that was just the beginning of his importance to the commercial success of the Ramones through twenty years of the band's existence, the twenty years following their breakup, and, given the strong brand he created, surely for the decades to come.

"He defined their look,' says Diodes manager and Crash 'n' Burn club founder, Ralph Alfonso. "All of a sudden, they've got these cool backdrops, he's got the signs, he's printing up their T-shirts. He took the raw clay and refined it. I mean, it's already there, but instead of Tommy Ramone sort of hand-drawing stuff, now you've got an experienced artist putting it together. It's like Brian Epstein, the fifth Beatle—that was Arturo Vega, right? Kind of the heartbeat that kept them all together. Because towards the end, I guess nobody was talking to anybody, but everybody talks to Arturo."

"His influence was huge," says John Holmstrom. "The Ramones had an art director. Their posters look slick. You look at most band posters that are self-produced, and they'll be very amateurish. But his image, with the eagle belt and the leather jacket, for the first poster, I was very struck by that. And they had that banner; that was stagecraft, professionalism. That was them being more than a bar band. They know what they're doing. They're not just four guys in leather jackets playing stupid songs. There's an art to this. He designed and made the T-shirts using that famous logo of his, and they split the money and

it was all cash. They sold more T-shirts than records. He was in charge of all the deals and it would've been quite lucrative."

"He was definitely the fifth Ramone," agrees Andy Shernoff. "He designed the logo, he gave them a place to live, he encouraged them; he was an artist. And he looked on them as an art project, and encouraged them as an art project; he's a very important player."

Arturo was also the band's lighting director. "Yes, and lighting is also a strong part of the band," explains Roberta Bayley. "The lights were kind of harsh and white and simple. He was called the art director of the band, which isn't a normal term that you would use, but his graphic sense and his artistic sensibility was part of the whole package of the Ramones. And then there's his devotion to them. I think he missed, in his whole life, maybe two shows, due to illness. He saw nearly every single show they did. And yes, they also made a lot of money from those T-shirts. It was a big part of what allowed them to survive."

"You wouldn't see their faces until song number three, because the lights would only be from behind," says

ABOVE: Vega's American eagle crest, emblazoned also with the immortal call to action, "Hey Ho, Let's Go," is as much a part of the Ramones' visual aesthetic as Joey himself, pictured here in attack mode with requisite foot-forward stance at the Hammersmith Odeon, London, October 2, 1978.

OPPOSITE: The Ramones with Arturo Vega in New York, 1976. Lenny Kaye recalls, "Arturo lived around the corner from CBGBs, which was quite a great perch, because after a show many people would gather there and hang out."

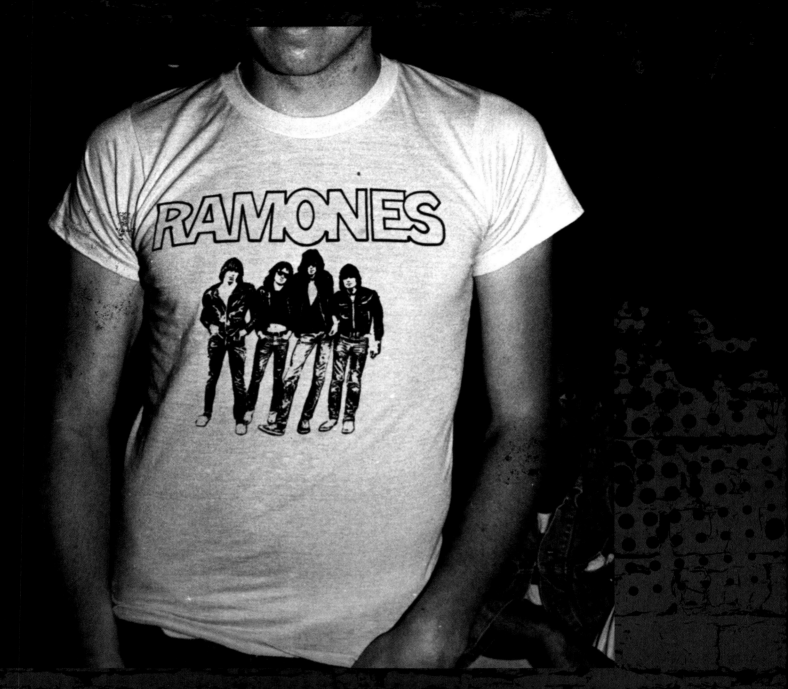

curator of the Ramones Museum in Berlin, Flo Hayler. "Arturo created all that. Arturo gave them their image. I think his biggest contribution to the band is the look he gave them on stage. Also what I think is interesting about the Ramones is that they were a prototype not just musically, but when it came to business. Today, nobody buys albums anymore, so bands have to find different income sources, the main ones being merchandise and live shows. Well, that's exactly what the Ramones did all throughout their career, relying on those two things: selling T-shirts and playing live. Because they never sold any records. I've never counted, but there's hundreds of T-shirt designs Arturo did. He came up with

a new design for every tour, and he was a pioneer in making special editions for single shows. He started the T-shirt thing to finance his tours with the Ramones, but once the Ramones found out there was a lot of money in T-shirts, they jumped on the bandwagon and pushed him to do even more shirts in various designs."

"Finally," says Flo, "Arturo was very important after the Ramones retired because he was the one who did the first webpage on the band. And so Arturo was the only one you could talk to after the band retired, in order to find out what was going on. So he was very, very active after the band retired. He only missed three shows! I mean, that guy . . . he was there every day and every night."

ABOVE: An early Ramones shirt.

OPPOSITE: "As soon as they got the right artistic people around them like Arturo Vega," notes Ralph Alfonso, "all of a sudden you see it becoming very polished." Johnny in the not-so-iconic red-and-yellow tank top, 1980.

ODEON HAMMERSMITH Tel. 01-748-4081
Manager : Philip Leivers
Barry Dickins & Rod MacSween for I.T.B. present
RAMONES plus support
EVENING 8-0 p.m.
Monday, October 2nd, 1978
STALLS
£2·50
BLOCK
18 | T59
NO TICKET EXCHANGED NOR MONEY REFUNDED
This portion to be retained   No re-admission

They weren't going to do it by sounding like the Ramones. And they tried not to sound like the Ramones for the next few records, and then they went back to sounding like the Ramones because they figured, we're not gonna have a hit record, might as well be the Ramones."

The second single was a swinging acoustic version of "Needles and Pins," while a late third kick at the can was "She's the One"—a typical hard-charging rocker with surf-music appointments. Not a single, but the album's enduring classic by far is "I Wanna Be Sedated," made special by percussion sweeteners and Johnny's choppy right hand hacking out the song's power pop chords. Marky recalls in our interview that, "The first song I ever recorded with them was 'I Wanna Be Sedated.' At this point, that album's sold about three million copies worldwide, because that song is played everywhere." Joey's

lyric for the track was inspired by the rigors of relentless touring at the instruction of Danny Fields and, in particular, a moment when the band was in London over Christmas with nothing to do but watch American movies in a hotel room.

"To me their most sensitive producer, beyond Tommy, who of course was an actual Ramone, would be Ed Stasium," notes Lenny Kaye, a statement that is exemplified by the bright tones of "I Wanna Be Sedated." "He caught their guitar crunch, their sense of propulsion, their incredible understated arrangement and segue from section to section. And because he has such a good engineering ear, he was able to make the records that have the most impact sonically. I mean, the first record is great, but by the time Ed came aboard, their sound had got more powerful from all the live playing and all the touring. But he

ABOVE: A whole book could—and should—be written about the band's epic tour with all-female heavy metal (punk?) band the Runaways. The Palladium, New York, January 7, 1978.

OPPOSITE: "Dee Dee was the biggest Bay City Rollers fan. I saw him after Danny took him to see the Bay City Rollers—and he was just floating. I think their song 'Saturday Night' was a big influence on 'Blitzkrieg Bop.'" Dee Dee at Cain's Ballroom, Tulsa, February 12, 1978.

"I WAS IN OUR LITTLE TOWN [IN RURAL ENGLAND], ON A NICE SUNNY DAY. AND THERE WAS A GROUP OF ABOUT EIGHT MIDDLE-SCHOOL STUDENTS HAVING LUNCH IN THE MAIN SQUARE. AND THEY ALL HAD THE BLACK-AND-WHITE RAMONES T-SHIRT ON. IT WAS LIKE THE RAMONES ARMY. SO I WALKED UP TO THEM, AND SAID, 'WOW, GREAT THAT YOU'RE ALL WEARING THIS SHIRT. WHAT DID YOU THINK ABOUT THE BAND THAT MADE YOU WANT TO WEAR THE SHIRT AND EVERYTHING?' AND A COUPLE OF THEM TURNED AROUND AND ESSENTIALLY SAID, 'WHAT BAND? THIS IS THE COOLEST SHIRT WE COULD POSSIBLY WEAR.' SO THERE'S A TRIBUTE TO ARTURO VEGA—THEY HAD NO IDEA THE RAMONES WERE A BAND."

CRAIG LEON, THE PRODUCER OF *RAMONES*

was able to convert that into the grooves of a vinyl record, with great guitar tones and a great sense of acceleration."

"Tommy had done his job as a drummer/producer, and wanted to see what else he might do," adds Lenny, commenting on the retirement of Tommy from the stool. "To be the drummer of the Ramones required a certain sense of being the drummer of the Ramones. And then Marky came in, from an early metal band called Dust, and had to simplify his playing, to match Tommy's thing. I think Tommy understood he had gone as far as he could as a musician within the Ramones and then as a producer, and it was time to see what else was around. He had very varied musical taste. In the end he had a bluegrass band called Uncle Monk. So I think he felt confined by his role, and didn't particularly want to spend his life on the road."

"The thing was, he wanted to leave after only three years," Marky replies when I ask him about Tommy. "He wanted to be behind the other side of the

glass, to produce, plus Johnny and Dee Dee would harass him and he wasn't really road-worthy. Producing was his calling. And I'm glad he was on board to produce, because I knew that he knew how to get a really good drum sound on the first album I recorded with them. So I was glad that he was on board for that reason. And plus we were friends. Like I say, the biggest song that we have is 'I Wanna Be Sedated' and 'Blitzkrieg Bop' is a close second."

Returning to the record, the opener "I Just Want to Have Something to Do" is another Ramones' classic, Joey skilfully addressing the theme of boredom, as he has done so many times in the past, but to a hypnotic mid-paced beat that is simple yet irresistible. Similar in its ragged drive is "I Don't Want You," while the Ramones catch some of their best speed, sonically speaking, on "I Wanted Everything" and "I'm Against It." The band positively roars out of the speakers with these fast songs, on what is probably the best-sounding

PAGES 78–79: The original lineup onstage at Cain's Ballroom, Tulsa, February 12, 1978.

record of their entire catalogue.
"Go Mental" and "Bad Brain" bring
the metal and "Questioningly" actually
sports lead-guitar licks, albeit of a
rudimentary textural sort. Closer to
real metal is "It's a Long Way Back,"
which ups the ante with the inclusion
of a twin-harmony lead, although the
band counters its musical complexity
with a lyric exactly fourteen words
long. The track is a melancholic end
to an album that is also somehow
thematically darker. Back in '78,
after Joey had just told Lester Bangs
of Trouser Press that the record is
their Berlin, Johnny laments in the
same interview, "I guess we just got
warped somewhere; a lot of pressure
on us. It's like, carry it out—go
mental. There's a lot of mental dis-
orders on that album. It's all just
piling up on us. Frustration? I'm sure
that's a lot of it too. We're feeling
a lot of pressure to make it. It's
been steady but slow. We've been
progressively getting bigger. But when
you see groups just pop up doing what
everybody else has been doing and

become big all of a sudden, when we
feel that we are one of the few groups
doing something original. . . ."

It would be remiss not to mention
the album cover to Road to Ruin, for
again, like Arturo Vega's graphic
design work for the band, John
Holmstrom's comic depiction of the
band helped listeners frame what they
were hearing.

"Johnny had shown me this sketch
that a fan gave them," Holmstrom
explains to me, "which is very similar
to what I ended up doing. And Johnny
asked me who I thought should do
the cover, and they asked some other
people too—including Bobby London—
and we both said Wally Wood. And they
contacted Wally Wood but he was in
poor health. So he suggested his
apprentice, but his apprentice did
it in his own style, and dramatically
reinterpreted the drawing and it was
this drawing of them standing on a
bunch of bricks in front of abandoned
buildings, and it looked like a comic-
book illustration. It didn't look like
a record-cover illustration. So Johnny

ABOVE: The Ramones, circa 1978, practice walking in the same direction, tougher than we were all led to believe, given the front put up, most deliberately by Johnny.

brought me up to their office, and he had all his sketches on the wall, and I was looking at them, and I'm going, 'Oh boy. If only Wally would've done what they asked. . . . They just wanted the drawing as it is but a little slicker.'"

"But the original artist had a lobster claw coming out of a speaker and a snake, and they wanted those elements removed," continues John. "So I'm like, 'Oh, okay, when do you need it?' He says, 'Tomorrow.' I said, 'I don't think I can do it by tomorrow.' But I did stay up all night, and I got it done, and I brought it up there, and Johnny is like, 'I don't like my face in it.' And I thought it looked just like Johnny. I did a good job. I really captured Johnny and Dee Dee. And Dee Dee is like, 'I don't like

mine either.' Joey didn't say a word. So I had to go back and re-draw Johnny to look more glamorous, and to me, more boring. To me what's interesting about the Ramones, they were like the Rolling Stones, even the Beatles, you know, kind of interesting-looking. They didn't look like fashion models. They didn't look like a boy band. So I changed that, and then I did the colorizing, but, I was so burned out, I did a pretty bad job. I just did a whole bunch of overlays and I drove the production department nuts. I see Spencer Drate once in a while and he still bugs me about it. But I remember being in meetings, and yeah, we're going to use the yellow logo on it and a black background, because that's shown to be the most commercial color combination. They had all these

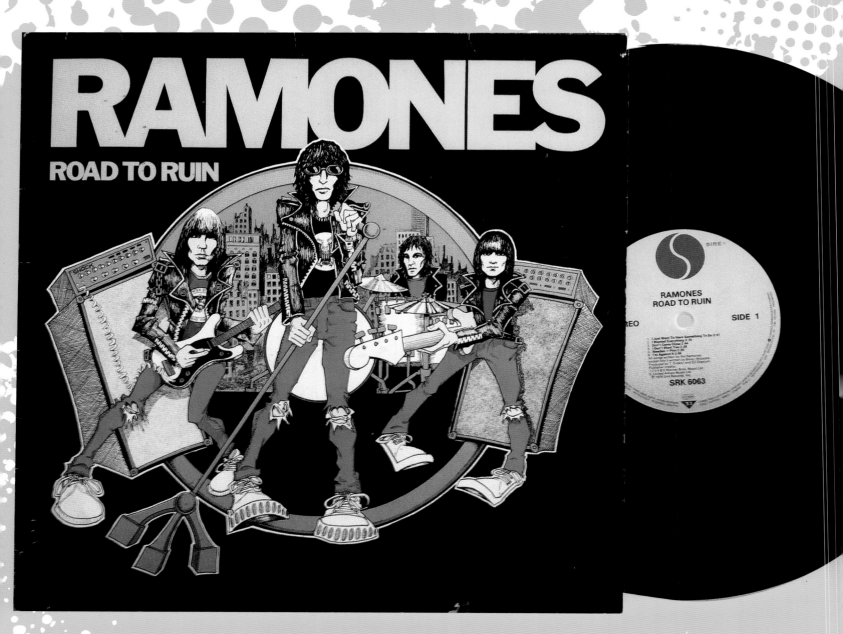

RAMONES
ROAD TO RUIN

RAMONES
ROAD TO RUIN

SIDE 1

SRK 6063

theories. But I think it was too slick for people. I don't know, maybe punks just weren't buying records. I don't know what went wrong."

"Who could blame the Ramones for altering their musical outlook?" asked *Trouser Press*'s Scott Isler when reviewing the album in November 1978. "Predictably enough, *Road to Ruin* (irony? foresight?) charts new directions. Equally predictable was that in attempting to change while holding onto their past, the Ramones would end up with an uneven record pleasing no one. By rejecting the role of new wave idiots savant, they become (just) another loud rock band. What the Ramones need is time to figure out who they want to be now that they don't want to be the Ramones.

Maybe we can look forward to their fifth album."

In closing, *Bomp* magazine in January 1979 summed up the tenor of the times when they called *Road to Ruin* "the record everyone thought would be 'make or break' for the Ramones, but really it's just another great album that won't sell enough to pay Village People's hairdresser bill unless there's a hit single. *Road to Ruin*, unlike the sun-and-surf mood of *Rocket to Russia*, establishes a tone of depression, uncertainty and alienation, which is understandable, considering the group's continuing tightrope position in the marketplace and the eroding force of the pressures on them. Please, America, give these boys a hit, so they can buy some new jeans and call their next album *Rags to Riches*."

ROCK 'N' ROLL HIGH SCHOOL

THE RAMONES AS SCREEN IDOLS

In 1979, the Ramones found themselves vanquishing Cheap Trick (and apparently Todd Rundgren, Devo, and Van Halen) for the role of fawned-over band in low-budget Allan Arkush movie, *Rock 'n' Roll High School*; the choice of the Ramones was aided by the fact that Sire Records had just been acquired by Warner Bros., overlord of the film. Provisionally titled at any given time *Disco High*, *Heavy Metal Kids*, and *Girls' Gym*, the movie was released on August 24, 1979, to generally favorable reviews and modest success, enough to prompt a 1991 sequel called *Rock 'n' Roll High School Forever*.

"That movie brought us to another level in the United States," recalls Marky. "Just like working with Phil Spector, it brought out the curiosity-seekers, who became fans after seeing us in it."

"For me, the movie is about how normal teenage life is somewhat mundane," explained Arkush. "What did you do in high school? Except for a few high points, you probably spent most of the time being bored. And the things that made your life exciting were often those involved with music. At that time in my life, in school, I really loved rock 'n' roll. And I remember finding (*Crawdaddy*) magazine at Bleecker Bob's and it was just like everybody thought about the music and was just as serious as I was about it."

Executive producer on the project was Roger Corman, which was enough for Johnny to leap in enthusiastically. But Johnny's energy, as he told *Trouser Press*, was short-lived once it got down to the actual work. "You're up there alone. I didn't like going to see myself in the rushes. By the third week, I just gave up. I don't mind seeing films of ourselves in concert, but you see yourself in the movies, and you just know you could have been better, but you don't know how you could've done it. You get there early in the morning and spend most of the day sitting there, waiting for your scene to come up. Then you have a two-minute scene, and you're all sleepy and wilted by that time."

"We were there three weeks, and they let us work on our scenes," said Joey at the time, in an interview with John Holmstrom. "I wrote that scene, the dressing scene. They asked us, you know, 'What is Ramones?' They had some things that were corny, things we wouldn't want to do. But they didn't say, 'You gotta do this.' They just said, 'How do you want it fixed?' Instead of making us look like fools, like all these stereotype exploitation movies . . . bands in the '60s, they look like assholes! Some people did it tastefully, but some, you'd see a band on TV and there was a band called the Mosquitoes and they looked like a bunch of stupid-looking hippies! It was all a take-off. In ours, it was all done tastefully, and that's why it works."

The bonus being they got to blow up a school. "The one in Watts was an abandoned Catholic girls' school. It didn't meet with earthquake standards and so it was gonna be torn down anyway. The majority of the movie was filmed there. After they blew it up, it was in wretched shape so they moved on to another newer school."

Afterwards, there were kind words all around for Allan Arkush. "He said, 'Decide how you want to come off in the movie,'" Joey continued to Holmstrom. "'Decide what kind of character you want to be, or personality.' He was

great! He made me feel real comfortable. Sometimes you feel real self-conscious being new at it. He tells you, 'Play off the other actors.' But it's weird for you. The weirdest part was when you have to do whatever your part is and you have to act it out, and there's about thirty people watching you do this, cameramen, the engineers and those people. And they find things amusing too."

Most grueling was the taping for the climactic concert footage. "We were there from about eight in the morning 'til about midnight in the Roxy. We must've done each song about ten times. From eight to like midday was one audience, and it was free, then from midday to like five or six there was another audience and that was about two dollars, and then from six to whenever, it was five dollars. At that time, we were working too. Whenever we weren't shooting, we were playing. I was really getting sick of 'Rockaway Beach' and songs like that. But now I look forward to those songs because I really like those songs anyhow."

"We did meet the director, Allan Arkush," Holmstrom told me, recalling his interaction with the film, and feeling glad to see his buddies getting to make a movie. "After they played 'Hurrah', he was there. And he told me that he was trying to describe the Ramones to Roger Corman; it was between the Ramones and Cheap Trick, to be in the movie. Allan was like, 'You gotta use the Ramones.' And to convince him, he showed them 'Mutant Monster Beach Party' from *Punk* and then Roger was like, 'Okay, let's use the Ramones.' And apparently that's his favorite movie that he was ever involved in. We were going to put it on the cover of what turned out to be our last issue, and Joey took all these photographs; he was taking polaroids all the time. But unfortunately we weren't ever able to publish the issue. They marketed *Rock 'n' Roll High School* as a drive-in movie, in the Midwest, where nobody had heard of the Ramones. People thought they were a made-up band for the movie and they reacted oddly to it, even though now it's looked at as a cult classic of sorts."

04

1980-1981

"A BUNCH OF KIDS IN A SANDBOX"

"A BUNCH OF KIDS IN A SANDBOX"

One supposes the Ramones' flirtation with the lush and balladic started with *Road to Ruin*, but the band as panoramic recorders exists, really, within the tight timeframe represented by the *End of the Century* and *Pleasant Dreams* albums, and more so the former.

The record's subplot—Johnny and Joey, and their sense of entitlement—exhibits an honesty that few other rockers would dare to show. Fearless of looking like sore losers, they spent more time railing at the industry and at dumb record-buyers as time went on—basically, acting like punks. But in some ways, they

had a point. In a just world, both of the above-cited slabs of aural delight should have crossed into some sort of RIAA certification. And when they didn't, a despondency of sorts set in the band, never to be lifted.

As fate would have it, there would be little post-retirement time for the band to reflect and reassess the validity of this period in their career. However, in the band's absence, scholarly fans have been taking up the cause, reassessing and elevating these two records, as the objectivity of greater and greater distance allows for.

PAGE 86: Virtually taking off the stage in 1980.

OPPOSITE: Joey preparing to beat on the brat onstage in 1982.

Too proud to admit it, or indeed, not introspective enough to notice, the Ramones had stalled in part because fans predisposed to punk were moving on to more sophisticated and varied evolutions of this music.

True, there was an industry-wide repulsion toward punk in general as it became violent and nasty, but there was also a sense of malaise associated with the Ramones specifically. It was felt that they weren't progressing, upon the evidence of *Road to Ruin*—which found the band stalemated commercially yet again—and also stalling with the critics for the first time. A double-live album with twenty-eight tracks, *It's Alive*, issued six months after *Road to Ruin* in April 1979 (only in the UK and Japan, where it was pared back to a twenty-song single LP), failed to make much of an impression either, save for reinforcing the idea that the band's best years were behind them, as the record celebrates the original lineup recorded at the Roundhouse in London on New Year's Eve 1977.

"The lesson to be learned," wrote David Fricke in his 1979 review of the record, "is that live Ramones in any form is required life-support for the '80s. *It's Alive* has particular historical value because it features one of the last band performances with Tommy Ramone/Erdelyi, documenting over three albums, the growth of the Forest Hills fire-eaters from the outside world's idea of a punk rock joke to a mature, powerful ensemble that does what it can do with no quarter asked, and none given."

The Ramones' fifth album, *End of the Century* (released February 4, 1980), marked a wholesale change for the band, who would spend upward of $200,000 recording with the legendary Phil Spector at a series of venues (beginning at Gold Star Studios in Hollywood), representing their first time recording away from the all-important creature comforts of home. Worrying to many was the loss of Tommy, but Ed Stasium was still there providing some continuity, and he actually wound up playing quite a bit

ABOVE: Looking particularly menacing in Amsterdam, February 1980.

OPPOSITE: Workmanlike ad for the UK-only version of *It's Alive*.

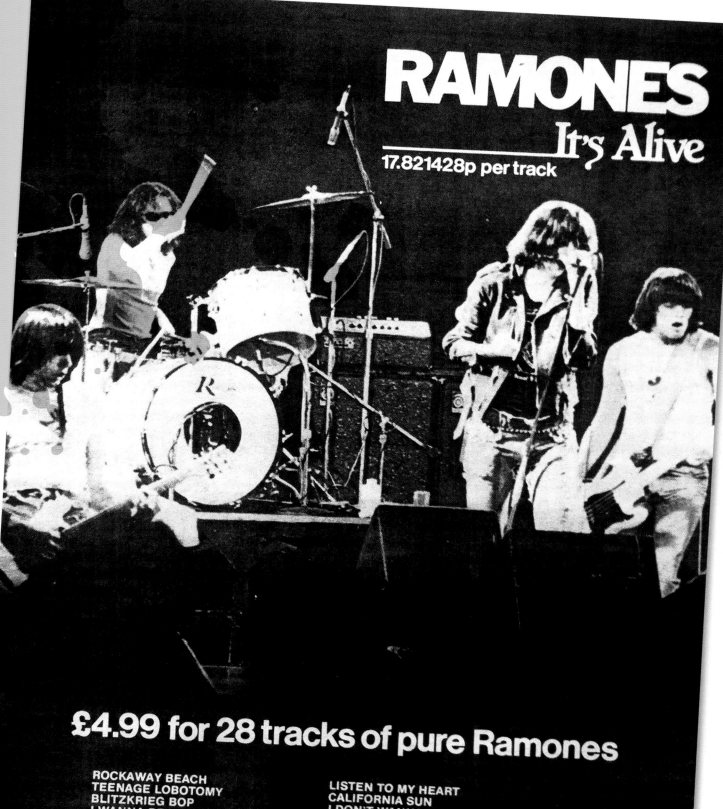

RAMONES
It's Alive
17.821428p per track

£4.99 for 28 tracks of pure Ramones

ROCKAWAY BEACH
TEENAGE LOBOTOMY
BLITZKRIEG BOP
I WANNA BE WELL
GLAD TO SEE YOU GO
GIMME GIMME SHOCK TREATMENT
YOU'RE GONNA KILL THAT GIRL
I DON'T CARE
SHEENA IS A PUNK ROCKER
HAVANA AFFAIR
COMMANDO
HERE TODAY, GONE TOMORROW
SURFIN' BIRD
CRETIN HOP

LISTEN TO MY HEART
CALIFORNIA SUN
I DON'T WANNA WALK AROUND WITH YOU
PINHEAD
DO YOU WANNA DANCE?
CHAINSAW
TODAY YOUR LOVE, TOMORROW THE WORLD
NOW I WANNA BE A GOOD BOY
JUDY IS A PUNK
SUZY IS A HEADBANGER
LET'S DANCE
OH OH I LOVE HER SO
NOW I WANNA SNIFF SOME GLUE
WE'RE A HAPPY FAMILY

SRK2 6074

SIRE

CALLING

Much has been said about the Ramones' influence on the UK punk scene, but when the band rolled through any given town across North America for the first time, a similar electric effect was had upon the music-minded locals. Witness the Ramones' first touchdown in Canada, for two nights in Toronto, September 24 and 25, 1976.

"Those shows were pivotal to the Toronto scene," recalls Ralph Alfonso. "In fact that whole tour that they did, the very first tour, was like an atom bomb going off in every city that they were in. Because as soon as they played Toronto . . . first of all, everybody was there in the scene, although there wasn't really a scene. Every outsider, every person on the fringe, was hearing about this punk rock thing. Teenage Head, the Viletones, and the Diodes were there. Basically anybody that was at that show, the very next day had a band. Like the story about the Velvet Underground, everybody who bought that album started a band. Anybody who saw the Ramones, started a band. But that Toronto gig established a link with Toronto, and with the two Garys, Topp and Cormier, who brought them back to Toronto three times."

"I'd never seen anything like it," he continues, remembering the Ramones' live show. "It was wild, crazy energy, fascinating, stripped-down—one song after another. And then from my perspective, when I was managing the Diodes, we got to open for the Ramones in '78 in Chicago; it was a triple bill: Diodes, Runaways, and the Ramones, at the Agora Ballroom. It was quite notable, because Diodes were allowed to have an encore. Usually the opening act, you got forty-five

ABOVE: Johnny backstage in Toronto.

minutes, you get out, right? And then Joey, the second time they came into town, when we had the Crash 'n' Burn club, we closed the club and had sort of a private party-cum-showcase, and every band played the party. The Ramones and Danny Fields were hanging out, to see how the Viletones did their thing. And I think the Dead Boys were the Ramones' opening act at that time, so Cheetah Chrome got on stage with the Viletones. Then when the Diodes played Max's Kansas City, the big showcase for CBS New York, Dee Dee Ramone came out, and I have a photo of him and the singer of the Diodes hanging out backstage. So there was interaction between the two bands, Diodes and Ramones. But basically, if the Ramones hadn't played the New Yorker, there would probably be no Toronto punk scene as we know it. There would've been, but it wouldn't have galvanized as quickly. Because in the beginning, it was like a clarion call, and everybody shows up. In 1978—79, with the Diodes, we did this quick little tour of the East Coast and it was the same thing,

NEAR RIGHT: Paul Robinson, lead singer for The Diodes. The band's self-titled debut from 1977 is a well-recorded, considerably heavy-rocking major label punk classic inspired by the Ramones' debut and the band's live gigs in Toronto.

FAR RIGHT: Johnny on stage in Toronto, shot by local legend Don Pyle, who has compiled a book of his fine punk photography from venues all around Toronto called *Trouble in the Camera Club*.

BELOW RIGHT: Ralph Alfonso, out of shot, chatting to the band in their hotel room upon arrival in Toronto.

Every city we hit, like Boston, everybody shows up. And years later you see what happened to some of them."

"In the case of the Viletones and Diodes, I think, yes," affirms Alfonso, asked whether Toronto bands changed their sound after experiencing the Ramones. "There was definitely influence. In the case of Teenage Head, they were around a year or two before everybody else. So their influences were more the Dolls, Flamin' Groovies, and that whole '50s sleaze thing. But the Ramones focused them as well.

Whereas, the Diodes and the Viletones were more from the minimalist Ramones trajectory. But the Ramones never really changed; they just perfected their formula. They didn't move it forward so much. The only thing that progressed was the production values. The basic template stayed the same. Which I think caused some bitterness, because they were seeing minor bands succeed. It's like Chuck Berry—you see other people take your building blocks and construct a skyscraper, and you're still stuck with the shed."

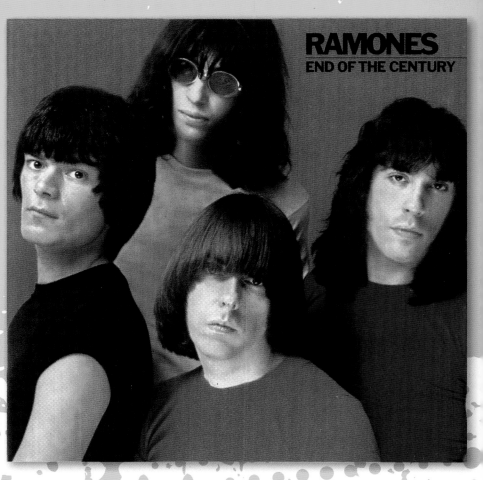

RAMONES
END OF THE CENTURY

of guitar on the album. The guys would escape the studios in about three weeks, but, comically, Spector would take another five months to mix the record to his exacting satisfaction, and, according to Ed Stasium, essentially remixed it three times.

Not insignificantly, the four Ramones would be photographed plainly on the front cover of the record, in bright T-shirts against a cherry-red backdrop, at the suggestion of top photographer Mick Rock. "Me and John wanted to wear our leather jackets," recalls Marky in conversation. "Dee Dee and Joey wanted a change, and they wanted to do T-shirts. And our manager wanted to do T-shirts. So we were outvoted. But yeah, vice versa, the inside sleeve was the one that should've been the cover."

"Phil Spector's one of the great rock 'n' roll producers of all time," said Joey to *Creem*'s Mitch Cohen in June 1980. "It's just that he didn't have anything to work with since the early '60s. . . . A lot of people think that maybe he dominated us, that he had total control, but it was 50/50. All of us together, we all wanted the best record possible." Added Johnny, "He would say,

'You guys wanna make a good album, or you guys wanna make a great album?' Anyway, our record doesn't have his old sound. It's us."

No strangers to creating band-width through overdubs, the Ramones succumbed to extra rounds of that with Spector, known for his trademark "wall of sound," his extensive overdubbing, and percussion flourishes enhanced by echo-chamber effects, as well as his insistence on take after take.

The opener, "Do You Remember Rock 'n' Roll Radio?", is a tour de force of Spector trickery, including horn arrangements and keyboards. Johnny was forced by Spector to play his parts over and over for hours, and the sessions quickly became tense. Still, the Ramones are positively transformed, and as far as Seymour and Sire were concerned, transformed positively (albeit not to expected levels), with the record finding its way to Number 44 on the *Billboard* chart—the highest position of any Ramones album, largely on the success of this song as a single, issued four months after the album launch.

The track "I'm Affected" is heavy Ramones but wrought through the Spector damper, while the Lou Reed-

ABOVE: *End of the Century* album released February 7, 1980. Just as the Boomtown Rats, the Clash, and the Adverts were about to go "post-punk," the Ramones went "new wave"—because that's what it was called in the US.

inspired "Danny Says" is a ballad similarly made rich—its lyric addressing the timeworn tale of management demands pressed upon their charges, its melody and arrangement creating a poignancy rare in the Ramones' catalogue. "Let's Go," however, is pure Ramones' metal mania without much of a Spector trademark. The band even chuck into the break something akin to a quote from the Dead Boys' "Sonic Reducer" and, similarly, "The Return of Jackie and Judy"—a typical Ramones song on any other Ramones' album—finds Johnny citing the intro riff from the Pistols' "Pretty Vacant."

"Chinese Rock" (previously titled "Chinese Rocks") is a raucous sleaze-punk paean to the hardest of drugs—heroin. The track also has a history of its own. After angrily dispelling the notion that Jerry Nolan and/or Johnny Thunders of the New York Dolls and the Heartbreakers had anything to do with the penning of it, as they had claimed, actual co-writer Richard Hell explained in a 2005 interview with Mark Prindle, "What happened is really clear, and the songwriting credits can all be checked at BMI. The song is by me and Dee Dee, but Dee Dee did

75 percent of it. I mean, all I did was write two verses out of three. Dee Dee wrote the music, the concept was his, he's basically responsible for it. But he brought me the song; he didn't even know Johnny and Jerry, but we were friends and he thought the band was great. And when the Ramones didn't want to do the song he said, 'Look, I've written one verse of this song with the chorus and it's about heroin; how about you write the rest of it and it's yours?' And that's what he did. I say it all the time: when I was in the Heartbreakers, everybody sang the songs that they wrote and I sang 'Chinese Rocks'—there are plenty of live tapes to prove it. Then I stopped performing it after the Heartbreakers and they kept playing it. That was their biggest song, so they wanted to take credit for it. Stupid."

Side two of the original vinyl opens with an actual Ronettes song—Spector putting aside any punk and pulling out all of his '60s production stops. Johnny had told journalist and musician Dave Bidini back in '79, "When *Road to Ruin* came out, 'I Wanna Be Sedated' was our unanimous choice for single, simply because we felt it was one of the best songs we've ever written! But 'Sedated' was never, ever released. They put out 'Needles and Pins' and 'Don't Come Close.' They felt that being sedated had something to do with drugs. On the new album, I wanted 'Rock 'n' Roll Radio,' but they released 'Baby I Love You.' It's all part of the fact that they're twenty votes and we're only four. We really have no control, but you can't do anything about it."

The truth is Johnny hated "Baby I Love You," commenting in the same interview for *Shades* magazine that the band isn't even on it, other than Joey, who croons along to a bunch of session players. For his part, Joey bemoans the low quality of his writing all over the album, while Dee Dee says he wrote practically nothing on it and played little bass. With the song making the Top 10 in the UK, the band found themselves on *Top of the Pops* miming the track along with—due to union rules—members of the BBC London Orchestra, while Johnny plays the castrated punk; as a Ramones' fan, it is painful to watch.

The rest of *End of the Century* is uneventful, mostly a curiously weak rendition of standard fast Ramones punk, save for "Rock 'n' Roll High School" added to the record as the moderate single from the movie, and slightly altered by Phil Spector from its original Ed Stasium production for the movie. Johnny was quite cognizant of the formula being applied, and realized that there was no point trying to go for a hit single with every song, because the heavier ones were going to be ignored anyway.

Perhaps focusing more on the traditional tracks, *Rolling Stone*'s Kurt Loder called the album "the most commercially credible album the Ramones have ever made. And they did it without compromising their very real artistic premises. Surprisingly, *End of the Century* doesn't sound like the end of the world overdubbed on twenty-four tracks in some airless Los Angeles studio. Though there's an abundance of overdubbing, Spector lets the Ramones speak for themselves. He's created a setting that's rich and vibrant and surging with power, but it's the Ramones who are spotlighted, not their producer. More than ever before, Spector has managed to conceal his considerable art and thus reaffirm it."

"I liked *End of the Century*; it was an experiment," reflects Marky in our interview. "I liked working with Phil Spector and so did Joey. I felt it was two walls of sound meeting together. He used brass sections, string sections, two or three organs, piano, any kind of percussion you can think of—it's the Phil Spector sound. I played different percussion instruments on the album; I brought in rototoms and told Phil, this is what I want to use on certain songs, and he agreed because they definitely worked well with the echo chamber."

"Phil always wanted to produce us, and we wanted him to produce us," he continues. "'Rock 'n' Roll High School,' 'Rock 'n' Roll Radio,' 'Chinese Rock' . . . there's a lot of good stuff on there. Obviously producing, Phil's the greatest, for what he had to work with in the beginning with his career. He only had two four-tracks and look at what he did. His strengths were obviously his production values, and his weaknesses were he could be a little temperamental. And I want to quell all rumors: he never pointed a gun at us in the studio. He might've some other place, but I was there all the time, and he never pointed a gun at us there. He did have a maniacal attitude, egomaniacal attitude, I should say. But, you know, a lot of geniuses do. And in my opinion, I don't think he's a murderer."

"He would yell and he would pound the board," says Marky, asked how Phil's legendary anger would emerge. "He would leave the room for a few minutes and come back and then get back to normal again. A lot of the times he would yell at his trusty engineer, Larry Levine, who was on all those great hits that he made before he worked with the Ramones. So it was—including the Ramones—like a bunch of kids in a sandbox."

A gun incident apparently did happen, but it was at Spector's

ABOVE LEFT: The artwork used for most variants of the "Do You Remember Rock 'n' Roll Radio" single, note that Joey is too tall for face-time.

ABOVE RIGHT: Howie Klein became president of Reprise Records from 1989 to 2001; Reprise would have Sire under its umbrella and so Klein's association with the Ramones would deepen.

mansion, where the band was held hostage deep into the night as Spector insisted they hear him play on the piano and sing "Baby I Love You." Tensions were exacerbated by the band itself scrapping, heightened by the others' reservations about Marky's fit for the Ramones plus their aggravation at his drinking (much of it in boozy bonding with Phil), along with Dee Dee's drinking and smack habit. Also causing problems was Phil's obsession with Joey's voice at the near-complete expense of the rest of the band, with Phil telling Joey he was going to make him the next Buddy Holly.

"He wasn't a pleasant person," Johnny told *Rolling Stone* journalist Colin Devenish in 2002. "He was nice to us, but he's just so horrible to everyone else around. I hear that he's pleasant now——it must have been the abuses he was going through personally, you know, substance abuses or something. I'm not sure what. There were demons inside of him. I had a hard time. My father died in the middle of the album, and that along with Phil's basic unpleasantness . . . it was hard. He was trying to separate Joey from the rest of the band constantly. 'Joey, Joey, Joey.'"

All told, Johnny and Dee Dee hated the experience, Marky guzzled wine with Phil and drove around in his Cadillac, and Joey enjoyed all the attention.

"It was great working with somebody like Phil," said Joey, somewhat incredulously, to Warren Kinsella in an interview for *Music Express* at the time. "He's a real rock 'n' roll producer. So it just worked out great. He's been wanting to do it for years, and we came to an agreement. . . . It was really relaxed. Phil's just a real guy. He's not phony or into hype or bullshit, and that's how we are. He's a legend until you meet him; you just see that he's a regular guy."

As a synopsis of the Ramones' positioning at the start of the new decade, *Trouser Press* magazine in January 1980 opined that, "The Ramones were once the great white hope of those who felt that rock was mired in some musical tar pit. These punk rock Brothers Four are caught in a tragic predicament: the music they paved the way for (without ever attaining mass popularity) has made the Ramones look a bit passé. Their catch-22 is that any attempt at musical diversification is a betrayal of their original precepts. The Ramones' sense of humor (their least valued asset) may help ease them into the '80s without provoking an anti-punk backlash. After all, without the Ramones, there wouldn't *be* a new wave."

After the hard graft that was *End of the Century*, Johnny and Joey were becoming increasingly bitter about not breaking commercially. Joey was more indignant from a music point of view. It seemed he was always on about the Cars and the Knack copping their bag, and then less obviously, bemoaning the continued success of Boston, Kansas, Foreigner, and Styx. For Johnny, on the other hand, not selling records was messing with his stratagems of retirement from music and a transition into film. His was always a grand plan thwarted by the cash cow not producing enough milk.

To complicate matters, everybody was boozing, save for Johnny, who kept trying to enforce a no-drinking policy. Worse was to come, when Johnny began seeing Joey's ex-girlfriend Linda Daniele in secret and then married her three years later, causing a rift through which Joey and Johnny barely spoke to each other for years and years. Joey was left wondering how they could continue to be the Ramones under such circumstances. Possibly, as a result of this situation, Joey never formed long-lasting romantic relationships for the rest of his life. He also became more cynical, combative, drank more, and his OCD worsened.

Despite it all, they kept it together. Marky explains, "because they liked the band. They liked the music and they liked playing. Now, did the animosities help the playing? Maybe it did! But I always felt that any kind of animosities you have towards each other, just keep it off the stage and play for the audience. That's why they're here."

A world tour was fraught with tension, with the band essentially sulking in silence—a survival mechanism that was probably the only thing the Ramones could agree upon, because showing emotion wasn't for rock 'n' rollers, even though Joey

thought it was at least fair game in songwriting.

Back in the world of logistics, Sire had rejected the band's suggestions for producers of the next album—Steve Lilywhite, or Tommy again with Ed Stasium—even if they got some good demos out of the sessions with Ed. "Actually, Joey played the *Pleasant Dreams* demo tapes for me," recalls John Holmstrom. "I was like, 'Joey, this is so much better; you should have released this.' And he gave me a funny look. Plus I think it's the worst cover they had, the *Pleasant Dreams*' cover. Just like *Road to Ruin* and *Rocket to Russia*, they were always coming up with something like the first cover, the first idea, and it never worked. And then they'd scramble to find something to put on the cover."

Still, despite all the attention surrounding Phil Spector and his guns on the *End of the Century* production, *Pleasant Dreams* deserves a re-visit; producer Graham Gouldman just might have struck a balance between locomotive guitars and ear candy that should have, on paper, kept rock fans stimulated enough to pass the Ramones out of industry-perceived parody into the realm of serious crafters of records.

Writing for what would become *Pleasant Dreams* began in January 1981, with recording commencing March 31 of that year in advance of the album's release date of July 20, 1981. The band was back in Media Sound, a former Baptist church on West Fifty-Seventh Street, and thus in possession of a cavernous room. Producing would be Sire's choice, Graham Gouldman, famous as bassist/vocalist for 10cc, but also a part of rock history in his own right for his penning of songs for the Hollies, Herman's Hermits, and the Yardbirds, most notably "For Your Love" and "Heart Full of Soul."

"I was sort of surprised when they approached me," explains Gouldman to me, "because I didn't really see any similarity between what I was doing, I guess, with 10cc. But from what I gather, the reason was more to do with the songs I wrote in the '60s, particularly for the Yardbirds.

OPPOSITE: *The Uncle Floyd Show* was a low-budget slapstick-type show out of New Jersey that ran from 1974 to 1995; celebrity musical guests besides the Ramones, shown here in a 1982 appearance, included John Lennon and David Bowie.

"I REMEMBER A MOMENT WITH JOHNNY. WE WERE PLAYING A FESTIVAL IN THE EARLY '80S UP NEAR BOSTON. . . . THE SUN IS OUT, AND WE WOULD JUST SIT BACK AND TALK ABOUT THE RED SOX AND THE YANKEES AND THE METS, AND REALLY, IT WAS JUST A BEAUTIFUL INSIGHT INTO JOHNNY AS A HUMAN BEING. I KNOW THAT HE KEPT A PRETTY TIGHT CONTROL OVER THE BAND, ESPECIALLY MUSICALLY. HE REALLY MARCHED THEM MILITARILY. THERE WAS A CERTAIN SENSE OF MARTIAL ARTS TO THE RAMONES, TO CONTINUE TO PLAY THOSE CHORDS, THOSE DOWN-STROKES, WITH SUCH POWER AND PRECISION. HE WAS THE TASKMASTER—AND THEY NEEDED A TASKMASTER."

LENNY KAYE, PATTI SMITH GROUP

They identified with the British invasion, the kind of rhythm-and-blues stuff of the Animals and the Yardbirds. That was where it met. I mean, they felt their songs were similar to mine. I couldn't really understand that, but I just remember nodding politely at the time. As far as I was concerned, we came from different places. But I said look, let's not jump the gun. Let's do two or three tracks, see how it works out. If it works, great, we'll carry on. If it doesn't, we'll say thank you very much and good luck. At the time, it all seemed to go very smoothly. I do know that afterwards, Johnny didn't like the album. I don't know about anybody else, but he thought it was a mistake, to have me do the album. But, hey, I did the best I could."

As had increasingly become the case, vocals took some time; Gouldman remembers, "Joey was great; very conscientious. He would quite often want to go over things again and again, to get it right in his head. And as a producer, I have to let him do that. And he was quite charming. I was in a hotel that was right nearby. It took about two weeks to do all the tracks, maybe even less. They were rehearsed, they were on time, there was no hanging around for hours and hours. They weren't as one might have imagined." He says, laughing. "So we did the tracks pretty quickly. There were certain tracks I actually played guitar on, but I had to play it exactly like Johnny would. I'd show him and he'd say, 'You play it,' but I had to play very restrictive, nothing fancy at all. We did all of Joey's vocals, in Stockport, in the UK, because I was involved in Strawberry Studios, 10cc's studio. He came over and did all the vocals there, and various other overdubs, spending about a week with us there. They put him up in a nice hotel nearby and he was on time every day and enjoyed working. He always looked very sort of frail and bent and pale, but he always seemed to be of a cheerful disposition."

"The first day was pretty much setting up and getting a good drum sound," he continues. "There was no subtlety involved; it was just getting it to feel good. And the room at Media Sound was great. A couple of weeks in New York, and then another week in London. I do remember when we were cutting the album, Joey would always sidle up to me and say, 'Is it too late to change something?' And that was the only time I said yes. But they were all very conscientious about what they were doing; they were serious. As it should be. I don't know why I even said that, but one maybe could've expected more of a casual attitude to things. But they weren't like that at all. They wanted things to be right."

Pleasant Dreams definitely sounds right, and self-assured, with opener "We Want the Airwaves" being one of the band's top-shelf songs of the '80s. Instantly one hears the fruits of the collaboration with Gouldman—the band rocking clean, hard and traditional enough, but with subtle stylistic touches, which are less obvious than those on *End of the Century*. The next track, "All's Quiet on the Eastern Front," is a sophisticated and percussive marriage of punk with Buddy Holly, while "It's Not My Place," "This Business Is Killing Me," "Don't Go," "7-11," and "She's a Sensation" further explore the band's complex relationship to the melodies of '60s pop, although less so to any sense of garage rock. Closer to garage rock, "Sitting in My Room" is a late-in-sequence gem, playing up the harmonies Gouldman captured so well—not too high in the mix, but consistently recurring.

"The intentionally moronic dynamite-charged pop of the Ramones is here and in fine form," wrote *Billboard* magazine in August 1981. "The maturity present on last year's smooth *End of the Century* remains, though the sound here is rougher. There also seems to be a hint of lyrical growth as shown in 'All's Quiet on the Eastern Front' and 'The KKK Took My Baby Away.' The quartet's last album, a Phil Spector production, was their highest-charting effort to date as it peaked at 44."

"When we did *Pleasant Dreams*, we wanted to strip it down a little more again, which we did," notes Marky, who made sure to come to work sober,

OPPOSITE: *Punk* magazine's John Holmstrom: "I always felt like Tommy was the general and Johnny was his colonel or lieutenant or something. When we first interviewed them, they were the only two that spoke. Joey and Dee Dee were silent. You weren't supposed to talk to them. That's why I tried to get a question to Dee Dee." Despite being "silent," it was Joey and Dee Dee (shown here onstage in 1981) who seemed to be doing most of the talking on the records, as the band's most prolific songwriters.

"WHY DON'T YOU TAKE IT OFF THE WALLS?:"

THE RAMONES MUSEUM IN BERLIN

Yes, indeed, there is a Ramones Museum . . . and coffee shop, and bar! But it's not in lower Manhattan, it's in Berlin, Germany—a fitting locale of sorts, given Dee Dee's roots growing up (biting the bullet, so to speak) on army bases up and down what was then West Germany. To make these things happen, it just takes someone to get off his butt and do it, no matter where they live. In this case, it was a Ramones' maniac from Germany.

"I used to have all the stuff at home," explains commando curator Flo Hayler, "and one day, my girl-friend said, 'Why don't you take it off the walls?' And I said, 'You're right. I should take it off the walls.' And then at one point, I thought, if I find a place where I can put it on some walls again, I'm just going to do it. And that's how it happened. A friend of mine said that a couple of people have space available and it's pretty much free, and I said, I'm just going to do it there. And I called it the Ramones Museum. There was no plan or agenda. It was just an accident."

A massive collector since 1990 (his area of expertise is the T-shirts), Hayler opened the first location in 2005. After having 10,000 people visit, he had to close it because the landlord "had to make space for a soap shop."

The new location of the museum, at Krausnickstr 23, 10115 Berlin (see ramonesmuseum.com for how to get there), has been in operation since 2009,

and has seen its holdings increase from the original 300 items to 500.

"It's open twelve hours a day," notes Flo. "It's important to be open in order for people to come in and see it. We get many tourists. A lot of them set out early in the day, so they try to see the museum in the morning, but at night we have events, so we're open a little bit longer."

Why the extreme fandom for Joey, Johnny, Dee Dee, and Tommy? "When I started to like them, nobody knew them and nobody liked them," says Flo. "They were very uncool. And for me, and I guess for a lot of other kids, every year you have kids of a certain age that hate their parents and hate school and want to be loud and revolt. So every year you have somebody who wants a soundtrack. And the Ramones provide that soundtrack for any

OPPOSITE & ABOVE: The reason Flo's archive is a major point of interest to punk fans the world over—646 square feet (60 square meters) of Ramones mania including these examples of Ramones fashion. Look but please don't touch.

thirteen-year-old, because it's raw and basic and simple to understand. Also it's very easy to join the Ramones as a gang. You can just wear a leather jacket and torn jeans, and you're instantly the coolest kid in school. And then you would gain respect because you were just so different."

As for Flo's favorite Ramones album . . . "The underrated Ramones albums are my favorite albums, actually—*Pleasant Dreams* and *Subterranean Jungle*. I think the Ramones have some of their strongest songs, some of the strongest Dee Dee songs at least, on *Subterranean Jungle*. There's a song called 'Outsider,' which is probably my favorite Ramones song, plus 'Highest Trails Above,' which is great, as is nutty, freaky stuff like Joey's 'Every Time I Eat Vegetables It Makes Me

Think of You,' another one that lots of people don't really know."

"It would take a while, but punk rock took over in all parts of the world," muses John Holmstrom in closing, proposing one reason why putting a Ramones museum close to the Berlin Wall makes poetic sense geopolitically. "I met with people from the Ukraine recently, and I learned a lot about the punk scene behind the iron curtain. Because, ironically, *Rocket to Russia* really was a metaphor for what happened to Communism. It was the music—that record was like a missile to Moscow. It was American rock 'n' roll music that inspired kids who did not have any freedom to want it. And I think rock 'n' roll is a pure expression of creativity and freedom and all the things these people don't have, but aspire to."

knocking off his drum tracks in four days. "I would say the equivalent would be working with Phil Spector, and then coming down to working with a guy like Shadows Morton. Graham Gouldman had written for the Yardbirds, he was in 10cc, and he had a lot of knowledge. And he knew how to get a great British invasion, I would say, punk sound on that album. It had a lot of nuances of that era. And we always loved that era, and all that was incorporated on that album. And we used the great Media Studio again, which we recorded *Road to Ruin* in. So we were glad that he was on board; he understood us really well. So yeah, great album—I love it. I even got to play kettledrums. It's the Ramones' pop-punk album; very British invasion meets the Beach Boys/Ramones. With the chord changes, the production, it's a very sweet album, maybe like our Beatles' *Rubber Soul*."

"I love 'KKK Took My Baby Away,'" laughs Gouldman when we talk about it. "I thought it was a great title." Joey's brother Mickey counters the popular perception that the song was a poison arrow shot at Johnny from Joey. Not that there was any shortage of gripes. Johnny wanted to keep the band slammin' for the hardcore fans, whereas the purposeful pop came from Joey, who also asserted himself on the record, making sure the credits reflected who was doing all the writing in the band, namely himself and the quite prolific Dee Dee.

Concurrent with the merger between Sire and Warner Bros., the band's five-year deal with managers Danny Fields and Linda Stein was up; they transitioned to concert promoter Gary Kurfirst, a Village fixture also from Forest Hills. Kurfirst managed the likes of the Pretenders, the Talking Heads, and Blondie. Although Joey and Dee Dee had been more impressed with another prospect, Steve Massarsky, Johnny—who didn't see reason for the change at all——had pushed for Gary over Steve.

Sire floated three singles from *Pleasant Dreams*, but only launched one, "We Want the Airwaves," in the United States, where the record stalled at Number 58 on the *Billboard*

chart. The insistence by the label on using another celebrity producer had failed a second time to change the toxic chemistry of the band enough to endear them to 500,000 American record buyers—the number needed to afford the band a gold record.

"I never really knew why they wanted to change from Phil Spector," muses Gouldman in closing. "That team seemed to work well. Maybe they were floundering. It's definitely kind of more cultured, that *Pleasant Dreams* record. But, you know, maybe their songwriting was evolving as well. The songs were more poppy. But no, they did what they needed to do in their inimitable fashion, and I hope I captured it for them. We were strange bedfellows, but I'm glad I did it. I have very, very fond memories of Joey. I remember we used to go to certain restaurants, and people were attracted to him. There was one place we went for lunch two or three times, and I'd go back alone, and every time I'd go back, it would be, 'Where's Joey? Please say hi to Joey. How is he?' He made an impression. He didn't do anything. He didn't start dancing on the tables or anything, but there was something very charming about him."

ABOVE: The opening track from *Pleasant Dreams* surely must be considered one of the highlight anthems from the band's '80s material.

OPPOSITE: The Ramones at a dinner in Bremen, Germany, 1980, with Linda Daniele.

PAGES 106–107: The Ramones performing at Top Rank in Brighton, UK on January 16, 1980.

"I HAVE VERY, VERY FOND MEMORIES OF JOEY. I REMEMBER WE USED TO GO TO CERTAIN RESTAURANTS, AND PEOPLE WERE ATTRACTED TO HIM. THERE WAS ONE PLACE WE WENT FOR LUNCH TWO OR THREE TIMES, AND I'D GO BACK ALONE, AND EVERY TIME I'D GO BACK, IT WOULD BE, 'WHERE'S JOEY? PLEASE SAY HI TO JOEY. HOW IS HE?' HE MADE AN IMPRESSION. HE DIDN'T DO ANYTHING. HE DIDN'T START DANCING ON THE TABLES OR ANYTHING, BUT THERE WAS SOMETHING VERY CHARMING ABOUT HIM."
GRAHAM GOULDMAN

05

1983...
1985

THE DEATH AND LIFE
OF THE RAMONES

THE DEATH AND LIFE OF THE RAMONES

The flight path of the Ramones around the making and release of *Subterranean Jungle* and *Too Tough to Die* represents, somewhat, the story of the times. MTV was becoming all-powerful, and there were both new wave-style synthesizer bands and heavy metal "hair" bands taking advantage of the new platform created by the channel. Furthermore, punk had become hardcore, with gnarly scenes at gigs across the UK and also, significantly, in Los Angeles. Casting a pall over all genres (save for the virulent new strain of punk) was the advent of electronic and digital recording techniques, which some bands chose to embrace, while others did not.

Broadly speaking, one could say that *Subterranean Jungle* represented the Ramones' dalliance with this hi-tech world. The first track on the album, "Little Bit of Soul," indulges most in the new genre, although—as with *End of the Century*—by the last track on *Jungle* we wind up with a mixed bag that left critics and fans on the fence.

But Johnny had had enough of that "crummy stuff;" he put his foot down for the "hardcore fans" (in both senses) and the following year gave them *Too Tough to Die*, which is less pop and less produced compared to the preceding records.

The years 1983—85 represent a fissure of sorts, a death of sorts, and then new life, made real in the flesh through the ousting of Marky and the hiring of the newly monikered Richie Ramone.

PAGE 108: Dee Dee looking omnious onstage in June 1985.

OPPOSITE: Not the legacy Joey intended: British hardcore fans, menace included.

Disappointing record sales into the '80s didn't mean that life for the Ramones was all doom and gloom. The band was nonetheless experiencing the world, although any joy they individually derived from the experience was not shared among them. The summer of 1980 found them touring Japan and Australia, followed by another long blanket tour of Europe. The next two years saw the band hammering America twice, along with Europe again, and on September 3, 1982, they took the stage at the US Festival in San Bernardino, California, opening the three-day affair on an oddball new wave bill.

After all the traveling, it was time to get back to their search for the all-elusive hit single, hopefully buried among the batch of songs they had cobbled together to form the next full-length album. *Subterranean Jungle* found the band legging it out to Kingdom Sound in Syosset, Long Island, every day throughout December to record, the producing spot this time going to Ritchie Cordell and Glen Kolotkin. Cordell had actually been

suggested by the band's first choice, Kenny Laguna, who was too busy to take the gig. Laguna had done the last two Joan Jett albums (with Ritchie)—*Bad Reputation* and *I Love Rock 'n' Roll* (both 1981)—and was managing her as well. Still, they used the studio from which roared *I Love Rock 'n' Roll*, Jett's 1981 smash album estimated at sales of 10 million worldwide.

Lacking new material, the Ramones went with three covers, and Dee Dee picked up most of the slack. "In most of the albums, except the last one, we always included old songs," Joey told *Billboard* in March 1983. "These are songs that we thought were great, and we could improve upon. We love all that stuff, the early '60s and the late '50s. Rock music in the '60s was exciting and made you think and made you a better person. It was a whole cultural thing. We were one of the originals, who put the excitement back into rock 'n' roll. Everything is big business now; there's no charm. The greatness of rock 'n' roll has been lost."

ABOVE: The Ramones got to watch their old buddy Joan Jett, seen here in '84, shoot to super- stardom while their early '80s albums stalled.

Two of the outside songs actually open the record, "Little Bit of Soul" and "I Need Your Love." These fit the historical pop milieu of the previous two records, but with modern production, which irritated the band's drummer to no end. "There was only one album I didn't like, which was *Subterranean Jungle*," Marky tells me. "I didn't like the producer, I despised the drum sound, but there were good songs on the album. I just didn't like the fact that he was using drum machine sounds that were popular at the moment, in '82, '83, that some of those new wave bands were using."

But in the same manner that the band eventually got to the punk toward the latter part of *End of the Century*, *Subterranean Jungle* hits pretty hard—even though the Ramones were now the last punks standing, at least from the original era. "What'd Ya Do?" is smothered in grinding rhythm guitar (it's no surprise Johnny was happy with his guitar sound on the record, which he rates a B).

"Highest Trails Above" is fast, metallic, and shockingly mystical, when it comes to Dee Dee's lyrics. Elsewhere, "In the Park" and "Time Bomb" are classic supercharged Ramones rock, Chinn-Chapman glammy of melody (inspired by the wonder-duo producers, Chinn and Chapman) but electric like Sweet as well.

Also mean and rumbling is "Psycho Therapy," which was an odd choice for a first single. The track represented a rare songwriting credit for Johnny (who co-wrote it with Dee Dee)—rare at least since the switchover to more individual credits, where it became all too clear that Joey and Dee Dee had been writing most of the songs all along.

"We did two videos off the new album," noted Johnny, in an awkward chat with Pam Kill that is featured in the 2004 documentary *Ramones: RAW*. "One is 'Time Has Come Today' and the other one is 'Psycho Therapy.' 'Psycho Therapy' is all finished and it was given to MTV." Johnny claimed that "MTV refuses to show it because it was too violent.

They wanted it edited, which we didn't . . . but the record company has edited it anyway and given it back to them, and they still said it was too violent. So that's it for that video. And it's the best video we've ever seen too."

The director of choice for said video was Francis Delia who, Dee Dee explains in *RAW*, was picked because the guys liked the "Mexican Radio" video he had done for Wall of Voodoo. Visuals aside, the kerranging anthem of a track was a missive from Dee Dee to Johnny, who needed some hard-core medicine to yank him out of his doldrums. The song quickly became a mosh-mad live favorite, with Dee Dee going so far as to say that the song saved the band.

The album closes with a similarly punky and combative rocker from Joey called "Every Time I Eat Vegetables It Makes Me Think of You," the percussive power on the track was courtesy of Marky, who would be gone before the sessions for the record were complete. Even though by this point everyone in the band was a mess, except Johnny, Marky's drinking had been deemed most unacceptable. Marky was subsequently ratted out by Dee Dee, who had found his stashed vodka and was soon waving it around for all to see, and that was that. This prompted Joey to make a phone call and quickly collar Billy Rogers to assume the stool for the band's rousing take on the Chambers Brothers' holler-along song, "Time Has Come Today."

Joey had trouble with the vocal on "Time Has Come Today," half-singing and half-talking his way through it, and Johnny was joined in the studio for the track by the Heartbreakers' Walter Lure doubling his rhythms. Still, with an ambitious adherence to the original's production touches, the band and manager Gary Kurfirst were hopeful that they had a hit on their hands.

During our interview, Marky sums up the turmoil within the band and his departure from it: "They were all different. Joey was very introverted, a nice guy. Dee Dee was an extrovert, a whirlwind hurricane, great song-

writer, the main songwriter in the band, and my best friend in the group. Johnny . . . well, he went to military school so he was very hard on them—not on me, which was good—because a lot of the situations were out of line. So it was good to have somebody out there to say, hey, look guys, this is our lives, let's make sure we always do 100 percent for the kids, which we did, which made sense. But yeah, Dee Dee liked to indulge in his thing, which was heroin, Joey was doing cocaine and drinking, and I liked drinking—my thing was just drinking. So I had to leave in '83. I wasn't an everyday drinker; I was periodic. The problem was that Dee Dee was doing dope. We were young, you know? I was three or four years younger than they were and I was enjoying myself. I had a good time for the five years, but then I had to leave. They told me to leave."

In spite of his nonchalance here, Marky's situation had been grave. He'd only recently passed out at the wheel of his '68 Caddy and crashed through a furniture store window; he'd had the DTs (delirium tremens—alcohol withdrawal) to the point of hallucination, and he'd relapsed quickly after a dim attempt at rehab. But there was more to his ousting than the drinking. Marky was seriously battling Ritchie Cordell over the drum sound, with Ritchie making little concession toward getting it to sound less digital, even if to be fair, the offense is varied depending on the vibe of any given track. In any event, the rending of the Ramones was to be depicted right on the album cover, with Marky exiled to a window seat on the underground train to nowhere, at the behest of Johnny, who had asked the photographer to plunk him there because he was on his way out of the band. All told, probably not one of the band's better jackets.

"With respect to *Subterranean Jungle* and *Too Tough to Die*, neither cover do I feel I designed as I was more an art director on both," comments Tony Wright to me. "I knew Gary Kurfirst as he worked with Chris Blackwell. I made a lot of covers for Island and was their creative

"'SUBTERRANEAN JUNGLE' SHOULD LAY TO REST ANY DOUBTS ABOUT THE RAMONES' VALIDITY IN A POST-HARDCORE WORLD. THE GLORIOUS WASH OF SOUND ON 'VEGETABLES' AND GUITAR SLUDGE ON 'OUTSIDER' AND 'TIME HAS COME TODAY' IS PROOF ENOUGH THAT THE ORIGINAL IS STILL THE GREATEST. LET THEIR IMITATORS DABBLE IN RADICAL SLAM-DANCING; FOR THE RAMONES, PUNK IS SUBSTANCE, NOT STYLE.

SCOTT ISLER, *TROUSER PRESS*

director in the '80s and '90s. I did the first B-52s cover under the pseudonym Sue Absurd. Gary took over the management of the B-52s, so it was natural when he needed something, he might turn to me. The subway cover: Gary was buying paintings by an artist who painted the subway and asked me to follow that idea for the Ramones. I was new in the US and asked the photographer George DuBose to shoot the band because he had been the person who had shot the B-52s." Wright felt that the shoot didn't really work. He comments, "That cover would be so simple these days with Photoshop but back then it was a pieced-together series of photographs and then a painting over a composite print."

"Time Has Come Today" was the second single floated from the album, but neither it nor "Psycho Therapy" would chart, with the album stalling at Number 83 on the *Billboard* chart. It would be back to the drawing board, but at least the guys now had a personnel shuffle to take the focus off their other problems.

While Joey, his brother Mickey, their significant others, and any number of resident and visiting rockers (including Billy Bragg— the infamous British punk-rocker,

known as the 'Bard of Barking'), indulged in the *Trivial Pursuit* craze of the mid-'80s, Johnny was busy getting his head stomped in a punk 'n' roll fight in August '83. His injuries were so severe that he required emergency brain surgery— much to the sadistic satisfaction of Joey, who was busy musing out loud to Mickey that he hoped Johnny's previous personality had been wiped in the process.

Prior to Johnny's misadventure, the band had been breaking in their new drummer Richie Reinhardt. They were pleased with his power, along with his ability to sing backups live and the occasional lead vocal as well.

Richie's first gig with the band was February 13, 1983, in Utica, New York; until Johnny's pounding, the band had been doing what they always did— playing for their pay, all across America and a fair bit of Canada. They were also unsuccessfully trying to sell *Subterranean Jungle* in a world now dominated by bands with better MTV videos.

Come time for a new record, the band welcomed back Ed Stasium and Tommy Erdelyi as producers. The initial rehearsals were done without Joey, who was in hospital with a

ABOVE: *Subterranean Jungle* cover art, with Marky clearly sidelined.

OPPOSITE: Johnny onstage on October 31, 1984 in Gainesville, Florida. Marky remembers how being on the road brought him and Johnny closer: "We would tour in the States, and John and I would go get the Yellow Pages book, look up the collectibles stores, go to the stores, and then we would collect all the posters and comics, that we liked. And the thing is at the time, I was into '50s sci-fi posters. I have about 300 of them and Johnny had a lot more. They were only like, $30, $40 back then and now they're like thousands of dollars. But that's what we would do. When we would get to a city, we'd waste away the time just looking for posters and comics."

BLITZKRIEG BOP

Here's a survey of interesting Ramones collectibles on vinyl; these items are chosen for variety across type rather than for sheer expense. The general tenor of Ramones collecting is that no particular pressing of any full-length LP from the band is in possession of a dramatic-enough storyline, or rarity, or graphic foible to push it to top tier. Rather, it's the myriad single variants that prevail, generally the earlier the better, with Japanese items particularly favored. Similarly priced at auction are your autographed LPs. This, of course, is a case of buyer beware, with detailed provenance and authentication being a necessary part of the discussion. Ranked highest in price to lowest. Enjoy!

1) "BLITZKRIEG BOP"/"HAVANA AFFAIR"

Fan favorite is this Japanese Philips issue, which reproduces the album cover, but with fiery red-and-yellow Japanese text on front: $500+. Dutch on Philips (b/w "California Sun," "I Don't Wanna Walk Around with You," live at the Roxy) is also very nice in black, white, and blue sleeve at $450. Also sweet is the UK issue on Sire (6078 601), black-and-white featuring live shots with cartoon bubbles, b/w "Havana Affair:" $400+.

2) "SHEENA IS A PUNK ROCKER"/ "I DON'T CARE"

Although less expensive than the Japanese "Blitzkrieg Bop," this Japanese single has a more aesthetically pleasing cover, featuring a black-and-white band shot splashed with reds and yellows. Philips SFL-2208: $300. Comments Ramones expert Jari-Pekka, "When I documented the Japanese singles on my Ramones homepage (ramones.kauhajoki.fi) in 2000, at that time I called "Do You Wanna Dance?" the most valuable of Japanese singles, with it already selling for around $500. I've seen some singles since go for $1,000. In April 2015, a promo copy of the Japanese "Blitzkrieg Bop" went for 600 euros."

3) LEAVE HOME

Japanese white-label promo on Philips has a four-page lyric/liner note/photo insert, plus a lurid pink and neon green obi with a small full-color picture of the band. Nippon Phonogram RJ 7208: $250.

4) RAMONES

Original US pressing (SASD-7520) contains misspellings, is designated "Marketed by ABC Records, Inc." and has no UPC code. Later issues are distributed by Warner Bros., with a new catalogue number, SR 6020: $120.

5

5) "GLAD TO SEE YOU GO"/"BABYSITTER" /MEDLEY OF "CALIFORNIA SUN" AND "I DON'T WANNA WALK AROUND WITH YOU"

This Italian 7-inch (Sire SAA 734) is odd, rare, and really cool-looking, and sells for around $100, with the rarer white-label promo fetching a premium. A razor blade printed with the words "punk rock" ensures its edginess. Jari-Pekka, however, has more of an affinity for the Irish singles: "You are really, really lucky to see any of those. There were at least five singles produced in Ireland between 1977 and 1981 and all of them are non-picture sleeves. What I, Hannu Jokinen, and Timo Pullinen know is that they were printed in runs of only 200 copies each for tax purposes: with that limited printing, the value was so small that you didn't need to tell the taxman that you were making these records."

6) RAMONES MANIA

The limited-edition double LP Record Store Day issue (RSD 2010) of this gold-certified Ramones hits pack came in vinyl that was cheery blue and cheery green, left to right, as opposed to one color on side one and the other on side two, which might seem a more likely combination: $100.

7) RAMONES

Original UK issue is Sire/Phonogram 9103 253. Black-and-white printed inner sleeve with lyrics: $60. "There were three versions of Ramones issued in Taiwan," adds Jari-Pekka, "plus one version of End of the Century and that's all for that country; I'd place these as some of the rarest full LP collectibles."

8) LEAVE HOME

Sire SA 7528. The US original including "Carbona Not Glue" was quickly withdrawn; still, it's not terribly pricey: $50; $70 if sealed. Perhaps even more sought-after is the UK issue of the album with "Baby Sitter." Says Jari-Pekka, "'Carbona Not Glue' was replaced on some countries' editions with 'Sheena Is a Punk Rocker,' but one Spanish edition includes both songs by mistake."

9) ROAD TO RUIN RADIO SAMPLER

Not the most expensive item, but just cool. This US promo item (PRO-A-756) features a proper printed cover, with the black-and-white shot from the album, as well as the words "Radio Sampler." Five tracks: "Questioningly," "Don't Come Close," "Needles and Pins," "I Just Want to Have Something to Do," and "I Wanna Be Sedated:" $30.

10) "SOMETHING TO BELIEVE IN"/"MY BRAIN IS HANGING UPSIDE DOWN (BONZO GOES TO BITBURG)"

Merely another one of the US 12-inch radio promos, because collectors like them, especially when the (usually and amusingly half-hearted) effort is made to stick some art on the cover—here we get a crap illustration of Joey: (PRO-A-2510) $25.

As a final comment, expert on Ramones vinyl Kristofer Forssblad Olsson offers the following: "I understand that this is not a list of the rarest records, but I want you to know that for most Ramones collectors, these are the three most wanted singles: "Do You Wanna Dance?" Japan, $400 to $600; "Do You Wanna Dance?" Netherlands, $350 to $550; and "Sheena Is a Punk Rocker" Spain, $400 to $600. Another nice record is the Japanese version of the live double album, It's Alive. In Japan it came out as a single LP album and with a totally different— and really great—sleeve."

recurring infected foot. Tommy remembered, "I would go to every show that they'd play in New York, and I tried to stay in touch with them as much as I could. They didn't communicate with each other anymore. When I left, things were still pretty much the way they were, but when I came back, they had formed camps and stuff. I worked with them for a few months. One huge difference is that when I work with them, I care. It's not a gig for me. Other producers just don't care. They look at it as just another gig. Do it and get paid. But to me, it's like, it's my baby. I really love the albums with Richie on them. I know a lot of people like *Too Tough to Die* but not the two after it, but I do! I think they sound really good. Richie's a talented drummer; he's very good."

"It's going to be different," Joey explained to Al Gomes of the *Providence Local* newspaper, pre-production. "It's real exciting. It's called *Too Tough to Die*. Not like any Ramones album. It'll be the best Ramones album yet. It's going to be totally diverse. It's going to have some hardcore, some traditional Ramones, a touch of metal, Jerry Lee Lewis—type songs. [Producing are] our original drummer Tommy Erdelyi and one of our original producers Ed Stasium. You know, put the old spirit back in. Not that we lost it, but it's sort of a reunion. Also, '84 makes it ten years, so it'll be like a real reunion."

The surly mood of the new record is established on the wrapper, even before the music starts to play. "After *Subterranean Jungle*, Johnny made me the 'official Ramones photographer,'" explains George DuBose to me in interview. "A year later, I got a call from Johnny asking me to do another cover. . . . I kept Tony in the loop on *Too Tough to Die*. I felt that I owed Tony one. I met with Johnny and Joey, and Johnny asked me if I had ever seen *A Clockwork Orange*. Johnny outlined that there was a scene in that film where a group of toughs mugged someone and the Ramones wanted to capture the essence of those tough guys in the film."

"I proposed that we photograph in a tunnel in Central Park," he continues. "I searched the various tunnels in the park looking for the smallest one, which would make the guys look bigger and more imposing. The tunnel near the

BELOW: A scene from Stanley Kubrick's 1971 dystopian classic *A Clockwork Orange*, inspiration for the cover art image on *Too Tough to Die*.

OPPOSITE: Joey sings his heart out at the University of California, Stockton, during a US tour to promote the new record in 1985. Tommy Ramone: "Joey was much more natural as a singer than as a drummer. He had a great voice and, I felt, a unique and strong presence as a vocalist. Things worked out perfectly once he became the lead singer."

MAKING YOU MINE

The Ramones, ever since they first put on the sunglasses, have been periodically, yet insistently, trying to teach us about the joys of garage rock and girl pop from the '60s. Here's an entirely opinionated list of the best ten send-ups of that music, at the hands of our musicologist punks—based on a fuzzy cocktail of popularity, critical success, fit for the band, and longevity in the hearts and minds of their base.

1) "CALIFORNIA SUN"
(FROM 1977'S *LEAVE HOME*):
The first and the best, "California Sun," made famous by the Rivieras, establishes the band as fearlessly pop, while they go about inventing punk before there were rules.

2) "SURFIN' BIRD"
(FROM 1977'S *ROCKET TO RUSSIA*)
"Surfin' Bird" sets the Ramones up as one-chord wonders before the Adverts; Joey necessarily carrying the melody on this Trashmen surf-rock classic— known for its babble of a breakdown it provided a fun moment, among many, at Ramones shows.

3) "TIME HAS COME TODAY"
(FROM 1983'S *SUBTERRANEAN JUNGLE*)
This apocalyptic, dramatic track known for its '67 psych rock vintage—"Time Has Come Today" gets a tough-as-nails update from the Ramones, who turn it garage with molten guitar tones and a snarling vocal from Joey.

4) "I DON'T WANT TO GROW UP"
(FROM 1995'S *¡ADIOS AMIGOS!*)
Poignant opener on what is a solid

if not stellar swan-song of an album, this Tom Waits/Kathleen Brennan composition comes off as autobiographical (and that's good and bad), and then tragically prescient. Musically, the Ramones make it their own as well, the band demonstrating, through the ease of the transition, why they are undoubtedly the inventors of the pop-punk that suddenly blew up big in the mid-'90s.

5) "DO YOU WANNA DANCE?"
(FROM 1977'S *ROCKET TO RUSSIA*)
Bobby Freeman's "Do You Wanna Dance?" was made famous by the Beach Boys in 1965, although both Freeman and Cliff Richard found success with the brief and catchy track. For our purposes, it's early, it's played live, it's a single, and it's from the Ramones' most beloved record.

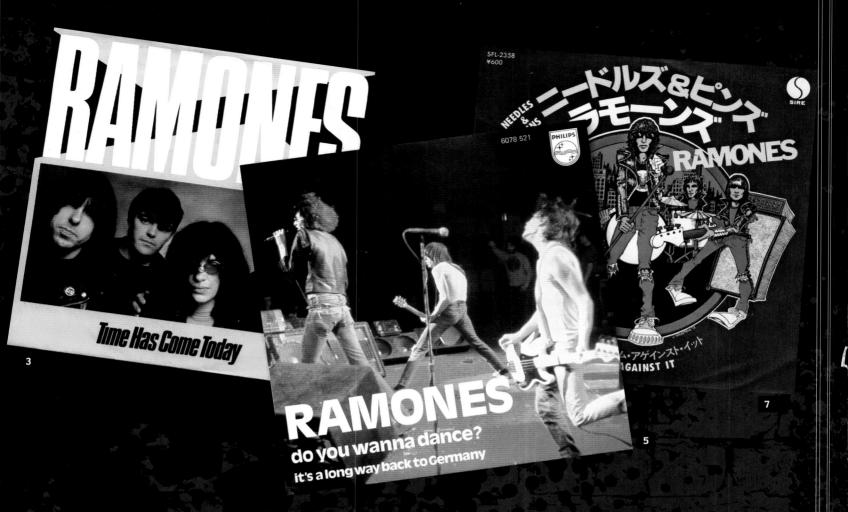

6) "MY BACK PAGES" (FROM 1994'S *ACID EATERS*)

Bob Dylan wrote it, the Byrds' popularized it, but it took the Ramones to turn "My Back Pages" into a spirited punk anthem, complete with Lemmy-fried bass and a young punk vocal from CJ, who draws up the blueprint for the rise of the Offspring, Green Day, Blink 142, and Sum 41.

7) "NEEDLES AND PINS" (FROM 1978'S *ROAD TO RUIN*)

An extensively covered song by Jack Nitzsche and Sonny Bono, "Needles and Pins" represents a brave shock on a Ramones album, namely a rare early acoustic ballad. But the recording is bright, the playing crisp and unadorned, with Joey selling the song with an Elvis karate chop.

8) "SURF CITY" (FROM 1994'S *ACID EATERS*)

There's not enough Dick Dale-vibed surf rock from the Ramones in the '80s and '90s, so it's cool to find a happy throwback to the first four albums on the otherwise somewhat oppressive *Acid Eaters* covers album.

9) "STREET FIGHTING MAN" (FROM 1984'S *TOO TOUGH TO DIE*, EXPANDED EDITION)

Provided as a previously unreleased bonus track when Rhino reissued the album in 2002, "Street Fighting Man" plunks on our list not so much because of its execution, which is a bit wobbly, but because it's a heavy step off the usual for the band. Fact is, Johnny hated this version, wanting Dee Dee to sing a punky lead vocal. Instead Joey picks his way through the challenging phrasing, with Johnny grumbling that it sounds like the work of a high-school band.

10) "7 AND 7 IS" (FROM 1994'S *ACID EATERS*)

Interesting choice and a competent enough execution of it, Love's "7 and 7 Is" finds the Ramones in Clash mode, setting up an intellectual parlor game around what the band might have sounded like had they embraced some of the fiery playing and politics of English punk.

Children's Zoo was the most effective. After rigging up lighting and smoke machines, we made a series of shots and took a break. After the break, I lined the guys up in the tunnel again and made a Polaroid photo with a Hasselblad to check the lighting. Fortunately, the front lights didn't fire, but the back lights did, and Tony and I were wowed by the strength of the silhouette produced."

"The crew had started to drop everything to fix the problem with the lights," corroborates Tony Wright when I talk to him about the shoot, "but it was obvious that while standing back watching for anything that looked effective, that it was a great image. So I said keep on shooting."

DuBose, summing up the fortunate event figures, "Roberta Bayley's album cover shot for the Ramones' first album was a photograph of how the Ramones really were. *Too Tough to Die* is a photograph of how the Ramones wanted to be."

The band recorded *Too Tough to Die* (named in homage to Johnny and his assault) once again in the homey environment of Media Sound, working in the summer of '84 in advance of the record's October 1 release date. Johnny took the bull by the horns and ensured the record would be heavier and less sentimental by writing on five of thirteen tracks, with Dee Dee mostly, who was much more inclined than Joey was to leaving out the boy-meets-girl/boy-loses-girl stuff.

ABOVE LEFT & RIGHT: UK record store ad for *Too Tough To Die* next to a UK concert notice, which also features upcoming shows from UK hardcore pioneers UK Subs and US hardcore pioneers Black Flag.

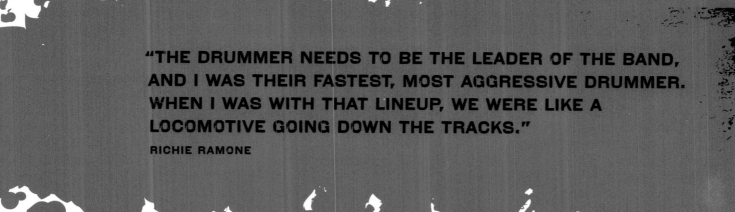

"THE DRUMMER NEEDS TO BE THE LEADER OF THE BAND, AND I WAS THEIR FASTEST, MOST AGGRESSIVE DRUMMER. WHEN I WAS WITH THAT LINEUP, WE WERE LIKE A LOCOMOTIVE GOING DOWN THE TRACKS."
RICHIE RAMONE

"Too Tough to Die was special," recalled the new guy, Richie, "because this was my first national act and here I was making a record with the Ramones. They had a couple of sleepy albums before I joined the band, and then we got Tommy Ramone back for this pretty dry-sounding, back-to-the-roots kind of Ramones record. And Ed's been around forever. Being a producer is just being able to sit behind the glass and know what to get out of the band and make them feel comfortable, and everybody felt comfortable with Tommy. When I got in the band, it was really cool, it was new blood, everybody's on their best behavior. There's a new charge, new drummer. The drummer sets the tone for the band. This band went through three different phases with three different drummers—and you can tell when it's my records. The drummer needs to be the leader of the band, and I was their fastest, most aggressive drummer. When I was with that lineup, we were like a locomotive going down the tracks. And around that time, '83 to '84, hardcore and speed metal were around, we started playing faster, and so we fit right in."

There's nothing hard about playing Ramones songs fast on the drums . . .

except for one thing, keeping the high-hat work metronomic, and usually quite fast. "You have to do a lot of eighth notes," says Marky when we talk about it. "Which is twice as hard to do than a quarter note. That's what the Ramones were about: down-stroking on the strings of the guitar, the bass, and the drums. That's what made the wall of sound. And to get that, I just used my fingers and my wrists basically. I listened to a lot of jazz drummers when I was growing up, and so I learned and knew it was easier to play rock. When you start listening to jazz, that's a whole new ballgame."

"Well, there is no technique," counters Richie, who instead of learning to bounce his sticks, just bulled his way through. "You build your strength up in the hand. In the beginning to develop strength in my wrist, I would play on a pillow. You know, a pillow doesn't bounce back; you always have to lift it off the pillow. And I think all drummers should practice that way. It develops the muscles in your wrist. Marky didn't use his wrist; he used his fingers. He cheated. I would hit it from the wrist, so it was kind of different. If you look at the videos, you can see what's going on."

Bullish indeed is tribal opener "Mama's Boy" and the rumbling "Danger Zone" is old-school Ramones punk verging on hardcore, while "Wart Hog" is shockingly hardcore, blasted rotten by the über-punk vocals of Dee Dee, who channels his inner army brat in the track. Late in the album's sequence, an ill wind returns for the band's thrashiest track ever, "Endless Vacation." "Planet Earth 1988" and "I'm Not Afraid of Life" are closer to leaden metal, with the latter featuring sweet ride cymbal work at the outset from Richie, who contributes his own hardcore song, "Humankind." "It's about people and life," Richie explains to me. "I write a lot about things that happen to everybody. Sometimes I'm afraid and I talk about fear. It's also about

people not treating you right, giving you respect or not giving you respect or always bugging you for something because you're somebody. It has all those elements."

The poppy and poignantly melodic "Howling at the Moon (Sha La La)" was the only single launched from this black leather record, with video director Francis Delia seizing upon the "steal from the rich and give to the poor" lyrics to create a New York City—based twist on the tale of Robin Hood. The song was produced as a UK single of sorts by the Eurythmics' Dave Stewart, who Gary Kurfirst had wanted to produce the whole record.

Overall, Tommy felt that this fan favorite, hard-hitting record should have been bigger; he later commented in 2003: "I was very happy when they

ABOVE: Pictured here with bandmate Annie Lennox in January 1984 is the Eurythmics' Dave Stewart, who produced for the Ramones "Howling at the Moon (Sha La La)" for use as a UK single. Management had actually wanted Stewart to take a stab at the whole record, but Tommy Ramone and Ed Stasium were brought back instead, and to great success all round.

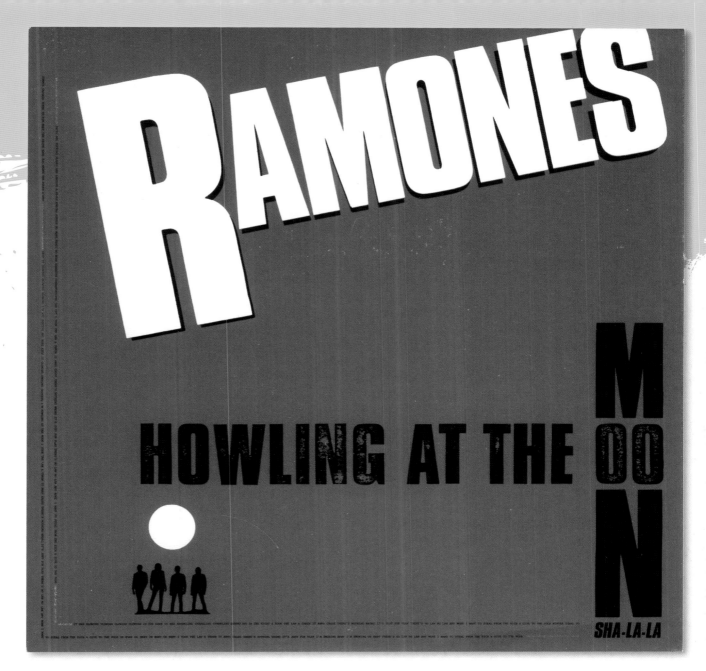

RAMONES

HOWLING AT THE MOON

SHA-LA-LA

ABOVE: Issued all over Europe, "Howling at the Moon (Sha La La)" wasn't even given a picture sleeve for its low-key American release.

PAGES 130–131: The Ramones rocking Club Manhattan, Spring Valley, New York in 1984.

called me up and asked me to be the producer. *Too Tough to Die* was a great opportunity for us to get together again. Too bad that record didn't sell a million copies, or I might have had a chance to do more albums with them. We worked very hard on this album. I spent about six months with them rehearsing for it. It was as if I never left, even though it had been six years. The band had changed though; they were not getting along with each other so that made a big difference, compared with the earlier albums. We had a slightly larger budget so we put in a little more time in the studio. I was heavily involved in all aspects of this album as I was with all the albums I have produced."

"We tried to make it harder and more raunchy," said Johnny about the album generally, when interviewed by John Richen in 1984. Essentially, it must be conceded that it was mission accomplished, even with respect to lyrics, which lean to the socio-political and generally heavy. Johnny explained, "The last couple of albums were kind of soft for us. The first five records were fine, and then came Phil Spector. That's when soft started. Things went wrong with Phil Spector. Things went wrong for the next three albums. [These producers] don't understand you. They all think 'hits' and that sort of thing. This new album we try to sound harder. That's the feeling we always try to get. Look at our first five albums. I think we're re-establishing ourselves with the kids who felt we had gone soft."

RAMONES 06

ラモーンズ

川崎▶クラブチッタ

9/6 (thu)　OPEN/18:00 START/19:00 前売¥5000(税込)

9/13 (thu)　OPEN/18:00 START/19:00 前売¥5000(税込)

9/14 (fri)　OPEN/18:00 START/19:00 前売¥5000(税込)

9/15 (sat)　OPEN/17:00 START/18:00 前売¥5000(税込)

9/16 (sun)　OPEN/17:00 START/18:00 前売¥5000(税込)

問い合わせ　クラブチッタ　☎044-244-7888

名古屋▶クラブ クアト

9/8 (sat)　OPEN/18:00 START/19:00 前売¥5000(税込)(ドリンク)

9/9 (sun)　OPEN/17:00 START/18:00 前売¥5000(税込)(ドリンク)

問い合わせ　クラブ クアトロ　☎052-264-

チケットぴあ　052 320 9
チケットセゾン　06 -309

9/10 (mon) OPEN/19:00 START/20:00 前売¥515

1986-
1992

"ALL HE CARED ABOUT WAS THE HARDCORE FANS"

Too tough to die but not tough enough to rise above their addictions, their petty jealousies, and their panoply of mental illnesses and social shortcomings, the Ramones found themselves once again unfocused after the hopeful hard-as-nails *Too Tough To Die* album failed to make a dent.

However, in 1985, the music industry itself was going great guns in Reagan's America, driven by MTV at its height. The boom spanned many genres, with heavy metal enjoying particular prominence. The Ramones, who had consistently railed against the metal credo for their whole career, weren't about to capitulate.

Nor were they going to adopt any of the other corporate ploys, be they visual, musical, or along production lines, to help stir some new excitement around their act. Indeed their next record outing, *Animal Boy*, mathematically adds up to a *Too Tough to Die* redux, but without the fire in the belly of a surprise attack. After that, if anything, the band's only concession would be an increase of melody back into their sound—the result being a wilderness of albums that lack concerted direction or anything to hang one's hat on, or indeed anything that could help the critics apply cogent descriptors to their sound.

PAGE 132: The Ramones found a welcoming fanbase in Japan when they went on tour there in September 1990.

ABOVE: Left to right: Debbie Harry, Joey Ramone, and Tina Weymouth at the Hollywood Palladium on September 20, 1990.

The band found themselves in the non-album year of 1985 with a song crafted for single release (a regular practice in the UK music scene, but previously foreign in the Ramones' world). "Bonzo Goes to Bitburg" was the product of the band's new UK deal with respected indie label Beggar's Banquet—the political track derides Ronald Reagan's decision to pay his respects at a cemetery in Bitburg, Germany, filled with the graves of several thousand German soldiers, including approximately forty-seven members of the Nazi SS. Reagan controversially described the regular soldiers as victims, "just as surely as the victims in the concentration camps."

The Dee Dee-driven track would serve, incongruously, as one of the most produced and melodic on the forthcoming *Animal Boy* album, but its title would be changed to "My Brain Is Hanging Upside Down (Bonzo Goes to Bitburg)" to appease Johnny, who was outspoken in his support of Reagan.

"That was one of the first serious songs we've ever done," Dee Dee told *Raw & Uncut* in 1986. "Like, Reagan's a good guy and everything; I don't want to knock him. But I thought it was pretty disgusting what the Nazis did. It was really awful. They were like the devils, and like Satan. The Nazis were like Satan. And for Reagan to go there

and go to the Bitburg cemetery, and to praise these SS guys, it's really disgusting. It was all politics. Like, I'll scratch your back, you scratch mine, that type of thing. So he was going to scratch the Germans' back."

Beyond this anomaly, the rest of the record, for the most part, played tougher and more hardcore. It was also recorded better, except for the muddy production of the aforementioned single and the equally muddied "Something to Believe In." Indeed, for his part, producer Jean Beauvoir— known to the band from the Plasmatics (also represented by Gary Kurfirst), captured the band solidly, albeit uneventfully, on the punk stuff.

"Each one of them had their own opinion," reflects Beauvoir when interviewed for this book in July 2015. "That's the interesting thing about a band like that. Johnny likes things very raw and Joey likes very

musical things; Joey loves piano and strings—all things melodic—and I like it all. So basically we went for a balance. Dee Dee was pretty open but he liked the punk stuff. He was pretty deep, as far as his thinking went. He was really passionate about music; we would spend hours on the phone going over songs. I think he was very satisfied with the end result and pretty diplomatic. As long as everybody got a little bit of what they wanted, it would work. Dee Dee had definitive lyrics and, as you can see, did a lot of writing on the record. As long as his messages were delivered and reflected on the album, then he was cool, as were the others. But Dee Dee was a great lyricist— and fast! He just had a speed. If there was something he had in mind, he could literally sit in front of you and it would just come out, and with everything that he heard in his head.

ABOVE: The Plasmatics making a video in the Lower West Side of New York, on July 22, 1980, featuring *Animal Boy* producer Jean Beauvoir, with a Mohawk, far right. "Gary Kurfirst was our manager, and he managed me as a solo artist as well at the time," says Beauvoir. "And he felt I could bring something to the band, add some extra little touches, and that it might be an interesting mix. I'd known the guys for years . . . and we all came from the whole CBGB/downtown circle. So I thought, you know, sounds like a great idea, let's do it."

RAMONES

BONZO GOES TO BITBURG

He was very clear and very precise in his thinking when it came to that. And then I would just embellish."

Standout tracks on *Animal Boy* are the irresistibly repetitive "Crummy Stuff" and strident, muscular opener "Somebody Put Something in My Drink," surprisingly supplied by the band's salaried drummer. "That's probably in the top ten of songs of their whole catalogue and career," boasts Richie to me, but expressing a truism, even if he cringes at Joey's faux-tough vocal approach to his good song. "That's a staple with them, and they played that at their last show ever, even after I left. We stripped it down for that album and had a lot of fun. We were using different people like Jean Beauvoir, who was great, a nice guy, really knew how to make records. And he worked well with Joey. The band would record the whole record in two days, practically. But then Joey went

to Sweden with Jean Beauvoir for like a month doing the vocals; the vocals always took the longest time."

"I had Joey do all his vocals in Sweden because I had an arrangement with Abba's studio, Polar," notes Beauvoir. "And that was where I did all my work for a couple of years, actually. Anything I did, I kind of insisted on doing over there. And actually, although I'd never seen one, there was a 3M digital machine there that was thirty-two track. I thought it would be a great idea to bring Joey to a different place and mentally get away from certain things. I wanted to share what I had going in Sweden; I just loved it over there. Sweden was doing some pretty happening stuff. We could actually take the record upstairs there, where they had a mastering lab on the top floor, and also a tanning booth, which I didn't use myself. Anyway, we would go up to

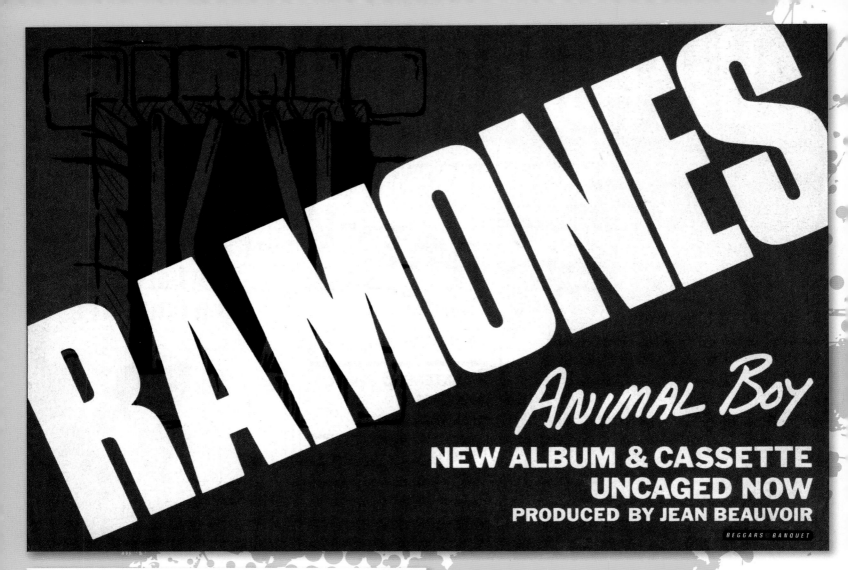

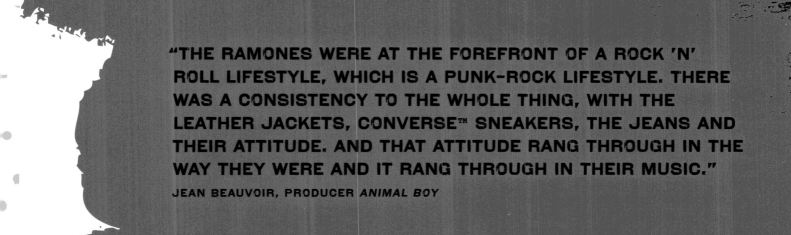

OPPOSITE, TOP: Small format UK ad for the *Animal Boy* album which is "uncaged now."

OPPOSITE, BOTTOM: The controversial "Crummy Stuff" sleeve. The single was issued in the UK only, but in 7-inch and 12-inch formats. Backed with "Something to Believe In" in all formats, the 12-inch variants also include the non-LP "(And) I Don't Wanna Live This Life."

the mastering lab where we could actually make a vinyl of something and bring it out to a club and play it."

As alluded to, the most enduring track from the album turned out to be Richie's rocker "Somebody Put Something in My Drink." "When I first moved to New York City in the late '70s, I was a kid and didn't have any money," explains Richie. "So I was dating the daughter of Franki Valli from the Four Seasons, and we'd go to nightclubs, and when people got up to dance, we'd steal their drinks off their table and drink them. And one night I drank one and started to feel weird, and it was spiked with LSD. So it's a very frightening experience. It's one thing if you take LSD and know that something is going to happen to you, but if you don't know you took it, you feel like you're going crazy. I told Dee Dee Ramone that story and he said, 'Oh, you gotta write that song.' So I have to thank Dee Dee. But Johnny got mad about 'Somebody Put Something in My Drink' starting with my drums. He thought that all the instruments should come in at the same time. I remember him saying, 'It's not a drum song.' He didn't like it when the drums started the song."

Animal Boy, issued May 19, 1986, finds Dee Dee, as noted, back to his prolific self, often co-writing with Johnny—while Joey was resentful of being pushed out creatively— a situation that is graphically illustrated by the amount of hardcore on the album.

This is shown most clearly in tracks like, "Animal Boy," "Apeman Hop," "Freak of Nature," and especially "Eat That Rat" and "Love Kills," which find quintessential street urchin Dee Dee turning in another set of his impossibly punk vocals, perfectly in character for a song about Sid Vicious—the Dee Dee across the pond.

"When Joey didn't want to sing, he didn't sing a song," recalls Richie, who himself sings "(You) Can't Say Anything Nice" on the UK B-side of "Something to Believe In." "Some things sounded better with Dee Dee singing them. Joey wasn't the type of guy that said *I have to sing every song*. If he knew someone could do better, then that person should do it."

Joey, who was boozing again, was only good for three credits on the album, a co-write on "Bonzo," plus sole credit on "Mental Hell" and the strident "Hair of the Dog." Both lyrics find Joey complaining, the former about his state of mind (due to the hard graft that is life in the Ramones, not to mention his recent breakup with his girlfriend Angela) set to a metal grind; the latter about a hangover, set to nondescript Ramones punk.

The mellowest track on *Animal Boy*, "She Belongs to Me," written by Dee Dee with Beauvoir, is practically a power ballad, with its keyboard washes and Bruce Hornsby piano. But a close second is the synthesizer-softened "Something to Believe In," which is arranged much like "Bonzo Goes to Bitburg" (with similar complicated UK origins), and was issued as a single in the USA, accompanied by an incendiary video that makes fun of the USA for Africa benefit event *Hands Across America* through the device of "Ramones Aid." Really glossy for the band and therefore commendably new, the single didn't do much for the record at large, which stalled at Number 147 on the *Billboard* chart—a slight improvement over its predecessor's Number 171 showing.

It is interesting to note that, now that the credits were clearly demarcated, Johnny was getting himself represented more than Joey, seemingly—and much to the chagrin of Joey at the time—through the monopolizing of Dee Dee's collaborative attention.

This was true to character, figures Richie: "Johnny did his thing; he was very mysterious, he watched the money, ran it like a top. And on tour, he wasn't a party guy who hung out after the shows. Basically you saw him on stage and when we were traveling. I don't like to talk weird things about people who have passed on. When they can't answer, I don't think it's fair. But we all know about John. They called him the führer and all this shit. But all that doesn't matter. This was a pro band. When it came time to do our show, we did our show, no matter what fighting or fistfighting was going on, or what we were saying to each other or who hated who. We knew for that one hour that the kids bought their tickets, we were going to give 'em their money's worth."

The Ramones' promotional campaign for *Animal Boy* saw the band on tour, blanketing the USA again, but not neglecting the UK either. New, however, was a visit for two shows to Brazil and one show in Argentina at the beginning of 1987. After this, a few more US dates ensued before they left the road to record again in April, this time with local punk acquaintance Daniel Rey producing.

Completely untested, Rey was this year's new idea for shaking things up. "I was just hanging out with the band and working with them," begins Rey,

SOMETHING TO BELIEVE IN

when we talk about how it all came about. "I got along with all the members, which was rare. You either had to be on one side or the other at that point. I guess [tour manager] Monte Melnick got along with everyone too, as did Arturo. They'd heard some punk rock single that I'd made, and they liked the way it sounded, and they figured, let's give him a shot—we know him, we like him, and he'll work cheap."

"It was a short-lived studio in midtown Manhattan with great old equipment," he continues, remarking on the locale for the band's 1987 album—Intergalactic Studios. "They had been through a lot of turmoil, so it was a regrouping. Joey wasn't writing as much, but Dee Dee was writing. Punk rock at the time was very out of fashion and there were a lot of hair and new wave bands with synthesizers and stuff. Joey was trying different things, but Johnny just wanted to stick to his guns, basically thinking that all this other crap will pass—and it did."

"We try to stay true to what we set out to do," Johnny explained in '87 to Erica Ehm. "We just wanna play wild, exciting rock 'n' roll. We've actually got a little harder the last three albums.

ABOVE: Both variants of the picture-sleeve version of "Something to Believe In" use famous historic "sideshow" photos, playing up the *Animal Boy* theme of the source album for the song.

OPPOSITE, TOP: UK ad for the "Crummy Stuff" single featuring a dollar sign in the band seal.

OPPOSITE, BOTTOM: A 1986 show notice for Club Metro in Riverside, California, signed by new Ramones drummer Richie Ramone.

RAMONE$ AID

CRUMMY STUFF

NEW SINGLE

PRODUCED BY JEAN BEAUVOIR

BEGGARS ⊙ BANQUET

HANDSACROSSYOURFACE

What is Ramones Aid all about?

It's about people, people who care. We think the time has come for caring people, who care about people, to stand up and be counted. The Ramones are standing tall for every cause.

So please, reach deep into your hearts and deep into your pockets – let's make this the most significant event of the Eighties.

As Joey Ramone says, and he speaks for all of us, "IF YOU'RE NOT IN IT, YOU'RE OUT OF IT".

– KEN SENOMAR, Spokesperson.

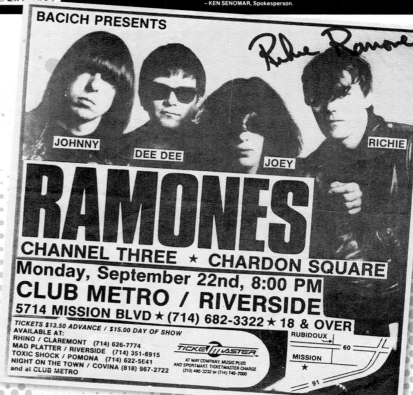

TOO TOUGH TO DRAW

3

6

1) RAMONES

Often imitated, its the first and the best. Confusing to me at thirteen years old, this cover didn't seem to so much express punk, as it did retro rock, or rockabilly, or even Quo rock. I seem to recall that it caused the buyer to pause—if I didn't get to *Ramones* slightly after *Never Mind the Bollocks*, *The Clash*, *New Wave* and *The Roxy London WC2*, it wasn't much before. "To me they were the perfect band," laughs John Holmstrom. "I wore those Chuck Taylors™ and those Converse sneakers all the time. I wore ripped blue jeans. I wore a blue jean jacket, instead of a black leather jacket—black leather jackets were way too expensive for me. But they were my lifestyle. And I thought they were hilarious. To me, it was a joke, but they did look like juvenile delinquents. Dee Dee looked like he would beat the shit out of you if you looked at him wrong."

2) ROAD TO RUIN

John Holmstrom's cool punk rockin' cartoony live doodle did much to set the goofy and approachable tone for the Ramones' particular brand of punk, as well as create an aesthetic for hardcore.

3) LEAVE HOME

I've always found this image appropriately punk, with its urban visual cues, along with its similarities with the wrapper on the Jam's *This Is the Modern World*. Plus the step-up to color, to me in 1977, subconsciously meant the music would be better too.

4) TOO TOUGH TO DIE

The type does as much to scream loud, bold, and back, as does the superhero stance of our heroes.

5) MONDO BIZARRO

Love the fresh colors, the association with psych, and the subtle suggestion that perhaps we should be forming a cult of the Ramones similar to the Deadheads. Says George DuBose, "The cover utilizes a technique that I "borrowed" (with consent) from Ira Cohen, the '60s hippie photographer who had photographed Jimi Hendrix, Janis Joplin, and many other artists in his Mylar chamber. Ira had lined a room in his apartment with DuPont's Mylar film and photographed the artists' reflections in that warping silver foil, producing images that had the visual effect of an LSD vision. It was bad timing as the cover for *Mondo Bizarro* would have been a better cover for *Acid Eaters*, the next album. Likewise, my shot of the Ramones sitting on a psilocybin mushroom smoking a hookah pipe à la the caterpillar in *Alice in Wonderland* would have been a great cover."

7

10

6) HALFWAY TO SANITY
Unadorned, color shot of the band, plus a smart "halfway" placement of title . . . what else do ya want?

7) BRAIN DRAIN
Here we have a great work of art used for a cover, the only hiccup being that it doesn't seem quite right for a Ramones record, unless one wants to get grim and think about mental illness. "I'm sorry to say, but I can't remember if it was a commission," notes Matt Mahurin, top tier fine artist. "But it's done with oil paint. I just sat in my studio and painted it out of my head . . . my brain draining onto the canvas. I did shoot Joey Ramone once . . . and that I remember!"

8) ACID EATERS
Appropriately psychedelic in lurid greens and purples, this one's got some surreal stuff happening if you look closely, although my favorite elements are the twin zippers and the fact that the hippie at the bottom looks like Hawkwind's Dave Brock!

9) END OF THE CENTURY
Hate to admit it, but I remember holding this thing in 1979 quietly kind of excited that the Ramones were trying to keep with the times.

10) PLEASANT DREAMS
I have a soft spot for the cover, because I like the record so much. Still, there's a nice congruence between the simple style of the thing with the sophisticated '60s-tinged

pop rock enclosed. When covers got downsized for CDs, this sort of layout excelled over busy photographs.

11) ROCKET TO RUSSIA
Says John Holmstrom, "Danny definitely was trying to imitate the first record. For some reason they hated the second record cover. I like it myself, but they hated it, and they wanted to go back. Everybody loved that first record. Danny definitely tried to recapture that whole image."

12) ANIMAL BOY
That's Legs McNeil in the gorilla costume. Legs was supposed to get credit in the liner notes for being the ape, but then Johnny didn't want anybody to know they didn't use a real gorilla.

13) SUBTERRANEAN JUNGLE
Bad lighting, Ramones on the cover twice, Marky sequestered and fake-looking, distracting tags . . . this one's just tiring.

14) ¡ADIOS AMIGOS!
Nothing about this absurd cover expresses or represents anything to do with the Ramones. "They did that cover because their manager, Gary Kurfirst, owned the painting," laughs Daniel Rey. "I think that's the main reason. He owned the painting and said, 'Hey, why don't we use this?' Which usually makes the painting worth a lot more money, so. . . . But the band didn't hate it. Kind of bizarre, but it's okay. Could have been worse."

We try to compromise less. At times you're pressured to compromise a little bit. We try to compromise very little." Added Joey, putting a positive face to the place of punk at the time, "Maybe it was different then in that there were a whole lot of bands. I think it's bigger now than ever. These are violent times. I mean, just look at the world. Just look at people. There's a lot of aggression out there. People are unsettled. Everything has gotten a little rawer and aggressive. We've just gotten more disgusted."

The resulting record, *Halfway to Sanity*, was in keeping with *Animal Boy*—namely Joey writing less than in the past, Richie writing a touch more, Dee Dee writing a lot, and Johnny getting in with his share. The wrench in the works was that this was

Daniel's first album production ever, and no one seemed to be listening to him. Joey and Johnny were still not on speaking terms, so Rey had to work with each of them separately, while Richie and Daniel, by Richie's own admission in our interview, "bumped heads; let's put it that way. There was a lot of head-banging and bashing going on. It's all under the carpet now and I try not to dig it up again."

Rey also commented to me about Johnny, "I don't think he was ever big on writing. After you're in the business for a while, everyone sorta finds their niche, and his was steering the ship, keeping the live thing together and making sure the albums were up to par. You know, if somebody brought in a song that was too out of character, he would just dismiss it, even if it was maybe catchy or something. At this point all he cared about was what the hardcore fans wanted—he never wanted to seem ridiculous. And so he was sort of quality control over the material. And also the money. He realized that if we spent $300,000 making the record, it would sell just as much as if we spent $40,000 making the record. So he kept that kind of stuff in check."

Also keeping Johnny happy were songs like "Bop 'Til You Drop," "Weasel Face," and "I Lost My Mind"—all co-writes between him and Dee Dee, all nasty and hardcore, the latter sung hysterically and histrionically by Dee Dee. "Worm Man" (Dee Dee's lyrics alone) and "I Know Better Now" from Richie, are whacked hard by tribal drums into tempered hardcore steel; even Joey's "Death of Me" is power-chorded and metallic.

Curiously comparative with "Bonzo Goes to Bitburg" and "Something to Believe In," are "I Wanna Live" and "Garden of Serenity," all four being sort of relaxed and poppy hard rock, with lots of production. "I'm really proud that me and Dee Dee pulled out a couple of really cool songs like those," reflects Rey, who during our interview shines some light on the writing experience. "Joey was very personal about his little songs, or his lyrics or ideas, whereas Dee Dee was very sharing. He was pretty fast too; he'd come up with like four lyrics and we'd just sit down to work, and we'd leave with four songs with chords and melodies. Whereas Joey would slave over an idea for weeks and weeks. Dee Dee was a little erratic at times, depending on what his mood was. During that time, he was off hard drugs. I think he was just on doctor-prescribed drugs and he smoked a lot of weed. But generally, he was just a sweet guy. He had his dark days, but he was always in fairly good form when we worked together. More productive than anyone else I've worked with."

"Dee Dee was a genius," adds Richie during our conversation. "Dee Dee was a poet. He had notebooks of words and he would write all the time, always about his private life. Because what's going on in your life could be

happening to millions of other people, and that's why people listen to it. If he was in AA or in the program, he'd write about his meetings. Or walking down the street. He just knew how to tie words together. Dee Dee wanted to call the album *Halfway to Miami*, but they wouldn't take that. But that just shows his genius mind."

A more sympathetic track was "Go Lil' Camaro Go," a nod to the old Ramones, but a little stiff . . . not a great song, although one made special with vocal contribution from Debbie Harry. "She is and always has been one of the sweetest people in the business," notes Rey. "She was just like, yeah, whatever you guys need. She came down, she got a kick out of the song, and it was a thrill for me. I was just a young buck, talking to Debbie Harry over the headphones."

Comments Richie on his slammin' "I Know Better Now": "As a kid growing up in New Jersey, what my parents told me to do, you may not necessarily believe it when you're young but when you grow up, you realize, oh, I know better now—that was right."

As for the dour and military hardcore of "I'm Not Jesus," he says, "That's about my Catholic upbringing, growing up in a Catholic home. On another level it's about people wanting something from you, when they write to you asking you these questions, 'Can you do this; can you do that?' That's why I'm saying, 'I'm not Jesus; I can't heal you.' People putting their hand out all the time."

Finally, despite all the rough and raw hardcore, captured stripped and simple by Rey, *Halfway to Sanity* shows glimpses of the real Joey, who wrote and crooned an uncompromised girl-group pop song called "Bye Bye Baby"; this was followed by an old-school happy Ramones chugger called "A Real Cool Time," which was issued as a single, alongside "I Wanna Live."

All according to plan, Daniel says. "Well yes, I think for a Ramones record we liked to balance it out. There'd always be two or three poppier singsong-y singles, and then we would try to have five really tough songs, and there'd be a few oddball covers,

or some really hardcore songs or something. So it was a balance."

If there was a nagging sense of the expected in the aggregation of styles addressed within *Halfway to Sanity*, the unexpected element would be the return of Marky Ramone to the lineup, with Richie gone even before the album hit the shelves in September 1987. In August 1987, Richie left the band over financial disputes; he was replaced in a scramble by Blondie's Clem "Elvis Ramone" Burke, who couldn't muscle his way through more than two nights before the band declared the experiment dead. So, briefly, the old gang was together again, but then it was Dee Dee's turn to "go rogue."

"I came back in '87, cleaned up, and have been sober ever since," explains Marky, about his return to the fold. "The thing is, we always cared about our music first. We never told our audience to do anything drug-wise. Particularly when I got sober, I would always say look, you're in a band,

what's more important? Achieving your goals in life, seriously, or drinking too much? And the choices always were continuing the music without the drinking. There's nothing wrong with drinking, but you should control it."

As for Dee Dee, Richie recalls, "He was functional, but sometimes he would have to get his stomach pumped, you know, before a show. But he never missed a show; he was always on. But at the end in '88 to '89, I could see that he wanted to do other things and leave the band. Which he did; he did a solo album but he was still writing for the group. Dee Dee was my best friend in the group. He was very jovial. Unfortunately he had drug problems. But if you have somebody that makes you laugh every day, keep them as a friend, because that's what he did for me. Every moment around him was funny. He was the main songwriter, he had a vivid and childlike imagination, and he put that into the lyrical content of his songs."

ABOVE: Dee Dee looking pure rock 'n' roll at the Paradiso, Amsterdam, on June 8, 1988.

"GARY KURFIRST USED TO [SAY] PEOPLE ALWAYS LIKE TO CHANGE AND TRY TO BE MODERN BUT THAT'S NOT WHERE IT'S AT. WHERE IT'S AT IS HAVING THAT ONE THING THAT YOU'RE KNOWN FOR. AND THE RAMONES MANAGED TO REALLY CEMENT THAT, NOT THAT THEY NECESSARILY PLANNED IT. BUT IT'S PROBABLY ONE OF THE REASONS WHY CONVERSE IS HUGE TODAY, OR WHY WE REMEMBER THOSE LEATHER JACKETS, OR THE POWER OF THE SIMPLE BLACK-AND-WHITE LOGO. THAT'S WHY PEOPLE OF ALL AGES, EVEN KIDS TODAY, ARE INTO THE RAMONES. AND I THINK IT'S UNFORTUNATE THAT THEY HAD TO PASS AWAY BEFORE THEY ACTUALLY GOT RECOGNIZED FOR HOW MUCH VALUE THEY ADDED."

JEAN BEAUVOIR, PRODUCER *ANIMAL BOY*

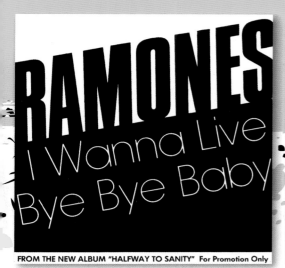

FROM THE NEW ALBUM "HALFWAY TO SANITY" For Promotion Only

ABOVE: Promo sleeves were never quite the same as the real thing, usually with less color or in black-and-white. These examples are typical with their bold lettering, ensuring that potential reviewers will not forget the name of the single.

Dee Dee was not the only one with issues. Marky was also returning to the ongoing problem of Joey and his OCD. "In the beginning, no one understood it. Johnny and Joey really never got along that well, so Johnny thought that he was doing it just to irritate him. But it was a [mental disorder]. Now of course we know more about it. So there were, again, petty animosities towards that. But he was afflicted with it, and later on I sympathized; it didn't bother me. But Joey and Johnny and Dee Dee grew up together, and they never understood it. They all thought he was doing it to irritate them."

Tensions aside, Marky remembers that the first order of business on his return was a standalone-soundtrack song: "They needed somebody quick. So they called me up—'We need you.' So I said, 'A second time? Oh no.' I was just kidding. But they asked me back and the first song we recorded was 'Pet Sematary' for the soundtrack and

the movie, plus the Christmas song that was on there. So it was a good comeback, that album. There was a lull for about three or four years, but then the 'Pet Sematary' song brought us back, because of Stephen King's involvement. That song, the way Dee Dee wrote it, there are so many influences on the Ramones from science fiction, horror, comics; you could say the Ramones were like a comic book. Throw that all together and it was a good fit for us, plus I liked the way Daniel Rey played on it."

"It was in between album cycles," recalls Rey, who would be replaced by the incredibly celebrated and intellectual Bill Laswell as producer this time around, although Rey still wrote and played on the record extensively. "It was like a homework assignment. We got the phone call, 'Write a song for *Pet Sematary*.' So Dee Dee ran out and bought the paperback and read the book or skimmed the book. He called me up and read me

ABOVE: Left to right: the "brudders" CJ, Johnny, Marky, and Joey in 1990.

some lyrics over the phone, and then I sat down and wrote the music in fifteen minutes. The next day we got together, made a demo, and the next week we recorded it."

Not a major song in the opinion of some critics, "Pet Sematary" was plunked next to a cover of Charles Barris's spirited and circus-like "Pallisades Park," made popular by Freddy Cannon in 1962. Nonetheless, "Pet Sematary" was a late-career hit for the band, much more successful than the album's other two singles, "I Believe in Miracles" or "Merry Christmas (I Don't Want to Fight Tonight)," all three being melodic and accessible but somewhat hair metal in arrangement.

"I really like 'I Believe in Miracles,'" Rey remarks in our interview. "I was a little weirded out by the mix of it, but I've grown to like it. The sounds are okay. There are some great songs, but we were still digging around for material, because Joey wasn't writing that much in later years."

Brain Drain (released March 23, 1989) was neither heavy nor light, but incongruously layered with '80s ear candy on top. Bill Laswell explained: "They really just do what they do. . . . Johnny was kind of serious. I mean, you're dealing with very limited 'everything' here. But he was a little serious, conscious of his parts. In retrospect, I made him overdub a lot, and looking back, it probably wasn't appropriate for the Ramones. But I was layering a lot of guitars, sort of like AC/DC. It was probably a bit much for the Ramones' sound, but I wanted to do something different and not just the standard punk thing."

"The melody came from the singer," continues Laswell. "I was more interested that the rhythm track was solid, and then I kind of overdid it on the guitars. As far as the melodic content, that was there. Considering the limitation of the musicianship, it was really tight, and very driving with a lot of impact. Strange band, with Joey's singing and everything,

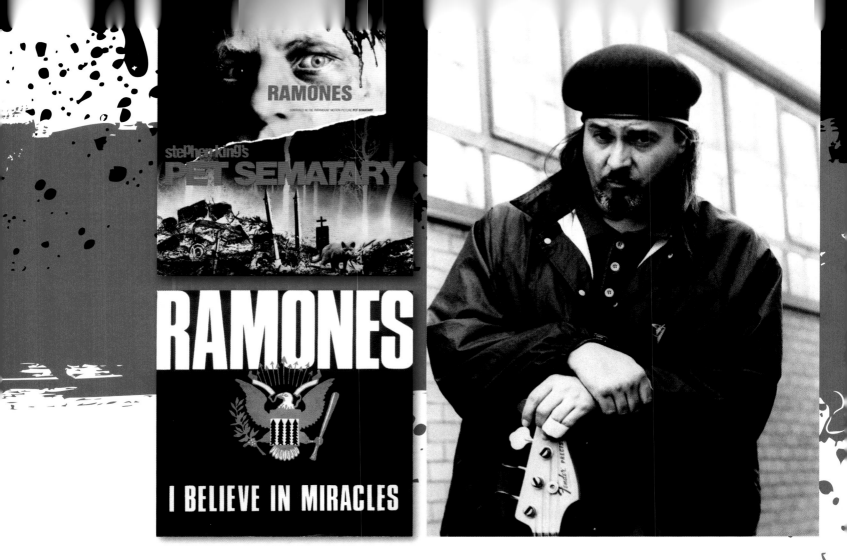

but it was like one unit, like a machine. They were a huge influence on bands that later on became much bigger."

The album contains some of the band's most simplistic songs, including the likes of "Punishment Fits the Crime," "All Screwed Up," and "Come Back Baby." Elsewhere on the album, there is the requisite dirty rockers skirting metal and hardcore, such as "Zero Zero UFO," "Learn to Listen," "Don't Bust My Chops," and one of the band's fastest and thrashiest songs ever, "Ignorance Is Bliss."

Rey co-wrote half the record, mostly with Dee Dee but a bit with Joey. "It's funny," he recalls in our interview. "Joey didn't know what he was doing, but what he was doing was very sophisticated. He would ask me to a play chord for a certain part, and I'd be wracking my brain trying to find this chord, and it would be like a minor diminished seventh, you know? He'd say, 'That's it!' I'd be like, wow, okay. He couldn't finger it or say

what it was on his two-string guitar he used, but he heard it in his head. Joey was more like a Brill Building typewriter; while with Dee Dee it was throw paint at a canvas, and sometimes it would come out very juvenile and it wouldn't work, and other times it would be pure genius."

"I was in there and played bass," adds Andy Shernoff when we talk. He also co-wrote two tunes on the record. "With the Ramones, you had to do it pretty quick, and so I was kind of in and out. This is right before Dee Dee quit. He came down to the studio once or twice, but I think mentally he was already out of the band."

"For efficiency more than anything," adds Rey, when explaining why he played some bass and guitar on the record as well. "It wasn't like freestyle jazz. It was all down stroke. I mean, Dee Dee could've done it, but it would've taken him two or three days and a lot of punching in, and headaches for the producer and engineer. But I could do it in a half hour. And Johnny, he would definitely

"WE'RE A PUNK BAND. THERE'S A LOT OF METALHEADS THAT LOVE THE RAMONES, BUT WE WEREN'T INFLUENCED BY METAL. WE WERE MORE INFLUENCED BY THE BRITISH INVASION AND THE PHIL SPECTOR SOUND AND YOU PUT THAT TOGETHER, PUT SOME AMPLIFICATION BEHIND IT AND PLAY FAST, YOU HAVE THE RAMONES. I KNOW EVERYTHING HAS TO BE CATEGORIZED, BUT WE WERE JUST A UNIQUE AND HEAVY IN-YOUR-FACE ROCK BAND. I MEAN, WE DID START A GENRE, SO I'M NOT GOING TO SAY WE WEREN'T PUNK. BUT WE WERE MORE THAN JUST THAT. WE WERE FUN, WE WERE PUNK, WE HAD ELEMENTS OF METAL, WE HAD ELEMENTS OF POP. MIX THAT UP, THROW IT UP IN THE AIR, AND IT COMES DOWN TO EARTH AS THE RAMONES OMELET."

MARKY RAMONE

go for the half hour," Rey laughs. "I didn't really work with Bill Laswell that much. We did all the rehearsals ourselves, pre-production. And then in the studio, he was really just there recording the band, more there to capture the sounds like an engineer as opposed to, 'Why don't we try it like this?'" Rey ended up being credited as "musical coordinator," because, he says laughing, "I think they felt guilty not giving me producer, not that musical coordinator came with a big paycheck or anything."

"It was rough only with Dee Dee," recalls Laswell of the experience. "I don't think Dee Dee even plays on the record. He came in a few times, and when he did, he said to me, 'I understand that you're working with rap artists.' He had done some strange rap song, 'Funky Man.' He seemed pretty out of it. Otherwise, no animosity and no conflict at all between the other three that I could notice. But Dee Dee came in and put everybody on edge."

The band would soon grab for themselves a shot of energy in the guise of new bass player Christopher Joseph "CJ Ramone" Ward. Of course, it didn't

hurt that the band had had an improbable hit with an unlikely soundtrack song, but bitching and moaning Johnny and Joey had long given up trying to figure out the music business. Their philosophy was that if kids were showing up at the door because of "Pet Sematary," then they would go to work and teach them a thing or two.

With Dee Dee gone for any number of reasons, including his exasperation and creative differences with Johnny and Joey, mental illness, cocktails of psychotropic drugs, or his budding career as rapper Dee Dee King—the band had to carry on. Johnny was his usual pragmatic self about the situation and immediately began auditions for Dee Dee's replacement.

Earlier, during spring '88, the band issued their first compilation, *Ramones Mania*, which became their first gold album, until finally their debut record edged along past that plateau in 2014. Before the band's next studio album after *Brain Drain* there was a contractual obligation to release a live album as well; March 1992's *Loco Live* marked the recording debut for Dee Dee's replacement, the aforementioned CJ Ramone.

ABOVE LEFT: The Ramones were now routinely headliners on bills with bands much heavier and more hardcore than their Beach Boys—influenced selves. This bill was for a 1988 show at the Celebrity Theatre, Anaheim, California.

ABOVE RIGHT: The Ramones are beloved by the Japanese more so as a lifestyle choice than a bunch of guys putting out records as their 1988 *Ramones Mania* tour demonstrated.

"Probably the worst Ramones record ever, unfortunately," laughs CJ when we talk. *Loco Live* did sound bad, with old classics played too fast and then egregiously patched up in the studio. CJ justifies the record to me, "It wasn't our fault though. We were forced to work with a producer who had no idea of what the Ramones should sound like. Besides that, Marky went into the studio and overdubbed all of his hi-hat and cymbal tracks, and stayed in the studio during the mixing to make sure his drum tracks were louder than everything else. Still, playing with the Ramones was a dream come true. It wasn't always great though. I took a lot of shit from the fans in the beginning, but Johnny always told me not to let it get to me. He really helped me out. I guess I learned a lot from all three of those guys, some good, some bad. But they were my boss. I didn't hang out with them. I would go back home after a tour and see the same friends I had before I was in the Ramones. I hate to say it but the one thing I learned from them was you can't trust anyone in the music business."

"They had the same technique," says Daniel Rey, when I ask him about the band's next studio album, *Mondo Bizarro*, issued September 1, 1992. "I guess they let in a little more outside writers. Andy Shernoff wrote on that; we did another cover. I think I played a little bit on that one." Rey was again writing, mostly with Dee Dee (not a Ramone at this point), resulting in the album's first single, "Poison Heart," another in a line of poppy tracks that pump along unobtrusively but briskly. Before the ink was dry on his songs, Dee Dee had to sell the publishing rights for some quick cash to get himself out of jail after a drug bust.

"We'd write in my apartment," Rey recalls. "I had a little studio. Started with a four-track and then went to an ADAT™ eight-track. We did the demos in my apartment and then when it came time to do the songs for the record, we'd pool all the demos together and everyone would listen to them and we'd grab whichever twelve or thirteen were the best. Dee Dee wrote the best punk rock lyrics ever. They come from the heart. He was very deep and troubled and he was the real deal.

SUZY IS A HEADBANGER

Ramones expert Jari-Pekka Laitio-Ramone has talked Ramones with all sorts of people, including makers of metal. Here's a sampling of praise from a few heavy metal heathens (obviously and similarly cursed with good taste in music), courtesy of Jari-Pekka's books, *Rock in Peace: Dee Dee and Joey Ramone* (2004) and *Ramones: Soundtrack of Our Lives* (2009).

"My dad wanted to have my brother and I go to New York. He told me I was in for a huge surprise. I was fourteen years old and was just discovering AC/DC and Black Sabbath. Father told me he had tickets to a special concert, the Ramones. I had no idea who they were. My dad's friend was the tour manager and he got us tickets for the show at the L'Amour in Queens. Finally the night of the concert came. The lights went out and a huge puff of smoke poured off the stage. The theme from the movie, *The Good, The Bad and the Ugly* came on and I was blown away. All of a sudden they came out on stage like a freight train and ripped through twenty songs in like thirty minutes. It was so brutal! The whole crowd was pogoing to the music. I never had seen anything like it. It was 1982. I will never forget it and will never forget the Ramones. 'I Just Want to Have Something to Do' is the first song I learned on the guitar and I couldn't stop playing it. 'Chinese Rock' . . . the bass pumps on that song so hard; Dee Dee really was hittin' it. And 'I'm Against It' is such a killer punk anthem, I would sing that song in high school and they called me a geek. The Ramones are the greatest rock 'n' roll band of all time, period!"

Frank Watkins, Obituary

"There will never ever be a band like the Ramones again. They are one of the best groups ever. I knew Joey always wanted the Ramones to be as big as the Rolling Stones or something; the Rolling Stones were a band Joey always looked up to. For me and as far as many other people are concerned, the Ramones are bigger than the Rolling Stones. They might not have been commercially as successful, but in my opinion their influence was so much bigger."

Mille Petrozza, Kreator

ABOVE: German thrash titan Mille Petrozza, pictured in Manchester, UK, in 2014. Petrozza cites the Ramones' influence on him and many of his compatriots.

"As a musician I've always been fascinated especially with how Johnny Ramone formed chords, playing downward strokes with his right hand. Some fans of metal music aren't so open-minded towards other musical styles, but many people really liked our version of 'Somebody Put Something in My Drink.' The original version contains such mega-cool vocals. Also the lyrics are great. I like the whole song, but somehow in those words everything is just going good. It was great to find a cover that our group of fans didn't expect. Anyway we didn't stop to think what was going to be their response. We did it for our happiness."
Alexi Laiho, Children of Bodom

"The Ramones are definitely one of my top five favorite bands of all-time. The Ramones and their attitude have influenced my songwriting, even though my bands Hypocrisy and Pain don't sound like the Ramones. Even though I was young in the '70s, I remember being pissed-off when Tommy left the band in 1978. I wish he would have stayed in the Ramones longer. I think Dee Dee was the coolest guy, just chaos and totally crazy. He even played with GG Allin!"
Peter Tagtgren, Hypocrisy

"The Ramones dealt with things in an excellent way. They kept up their harsh style, but I felt that they didn't take things too seriously. They played their music at high speed, with humor and with good feeling. Of their songs, 'Pinhead' was my first love. As a teenager I played it on my guitar, but I've never played their songs with any of my bands.

The lyrics of the early Ramones songs are a mixture of unique wit and humor. For example, the refrain of 'We're a Happy Family' works, even though it's so simple. If anyone other than the Ramones had done it, it would have been bad. Ramones music made you feel good. When you hear their music, you start to smile."
Marco Hietala, Nightwish

"The Ramones were and are like no other rock 'n' roll band I have or will ever hear in my life. Truly inspirational. I first heard the Ramones when I was growing up in Belfast at age fourteen. To say that they had a profound effect on my life is an understatement. They looked and sounded like no one else and I was instantly addicted. A few years later I was fronting my own band, the Almighty, who were confirmed as the support for the Ramones forthcoming UK *Brain Drain* tour. Here was a band we idolized who had a huge influence on us and we were going on tour with them! At the first show, in Leicester, England, we were excited and nervous. About four shows into the tour, Johnny came into our dressing room and asked us if everything was okay? 'Brilliant. Why do you ask?' He said that we seemed very quiet on the tour. We told him that basically we were a bit awestruck as we were all massive Ramones fans. Johnny laughed and told us not to be so silly. From then on we were on a massive high, hanging out with the band and crew at every opportunity."
Ricky Warwick, Black Star Riders

"Many metal bands found the speed and energy from hardcore and punk music, and the Ramones were one of the first bands to play really fast. They influenced tons of bands."
Jon Larsen, Volbeat

"As a songwriter, I always try to go straight to the heart of the people who want to listen. That's what the Ramones did to me. If the song was one minute fifty long, who cares? It was not supposed to be longer. You had a verse and a chorus, another verse and chorus, fine that's it, that's all it needed. The Ramones were so honest and from the heart. Plus the fact that Joey Ramone sounds like a singer from the '50s or '60s with that special vibrato, it's like he's in the wrong band at the wrong time, but you love it."
Dan Swanö, Edge of Sanity

His lyrics, his whole persona, was what it was all about. He was fearless and he was like a troubadour. Always moving fast trying to keep ahead of his demons. There's an honesty there that is very rare."

Daniel Rey and Dee Dee also collaborated on the similarly mid-tempo "Strength to Endure" and the metal-ish "Main Man," while elsewhere on the album, the band cover the Doors' "Take It As It Comes." "We did three nights at the Hollywood Palladium, which nobody does," crowed Joey at the time, to journalist Don Kaye for *Rip*. "And we got a letter from Robbie Krieger, the Doors' guitarist. When he heard our version, he loved it, and said that when we were in L.A., he'd love to come down and play with us. It was very exciting for us, because we're big Doors fans. Plus it was a historic coupling—he's the first musician we've ever let play with us in a live situation. A lot of really exciting things have been happening."

For the album, Joey also wrote with Andy Shernoff on the richly poppy pair "It's Gonna Be Alright" and "I Won't Let it Happen"—the latter being a near ballad.

"At the end of the '80s, I guess Joey started getting a little dried-up creatively and he needed a little bit of influence from other people to write with," explains Andy to me. "And he started writing more with Daniel and me, and also Richie Stotts, which is on the last posthumous solo record. We would hang out, he would present me with an idea or I'd present him with an idea, and obviously he had

final say. He had this kind of Japanese Les Paul Junior, which had three strings on it—three top strings, heavy strings—and they were tuned sort of open. And he would have a melody, go up and down the neck, and then he would have somebody else come in and sort of finesse it. Joey had started 'It's Gonna Be Alright,' and then I threw in a bridge or a chord or two, while for 'I Won't Let It Happen,' I'd given him a tape, and here we thought, everything else was typical fast Ramones stuff, and that one I'd written on acoustic and he liked it. He wrote some words for it and they ended up using it."

"Usually this would be at his apartment," continues Andy, elaborating on Joey's living space. "One time he came to my apartment, but it was usually at his place on Ninth Street, in the East Village. He bought three apartments in this old building. One was his original small studio, and then there were two one-bedrooms, all in the same wing. The biggest apartment was where he was living, and then he had one apartment which was like a hangout. He had some gym equipment in there, a running machine kind of thing. The other apartment was

ABOVE LEFT: Ticket for the Ramones at legendary music venue, the Refectory at the University of Leeds, UK on October 4, 1989.

ABOVE RIGHT: Chrysalis UK issued "Poison Heart" in this kaleidoscopic sleeve in 7-inch, 12-inch, and CD single formats.

used for storage, and then he rented it out to make some money."

The last track on the record, "Touring," was a leftover from the *Pleasant Dreams* days and pairs an amusing Joey lyric about the road with a reworked version of the music from "Rock 'n' Roll High School." Other highlights on the record would be "Censorshit," "The Job That Ate My Brain," and "Heidi Is a Headcase," which all possess the critical mass and energy of the *Too Tough to Die* album.

"They're just all about people and places that they've been to," notes Rey. "'Heidi Is a Headcase' is about some crazy girl that Joey met in a club one night. 'Poison Heart' was Dee Dee looking out the car window and seeing degradation on the street. Dee Dee also went to rehab, and 'strength to endure' is a term used in the program. They're all positive and life-affirming."

These tracks, along with the usual dose of hardcore pushed through a strong Ed Stasium production job, had critics calling *Mondo Bizarro* the best Ramones' record since *Too Tough to Die*. It also helped that Joey was publically declaring that he was clean and sober, and was singing and writing better than ever. Buoyed by success in South America, he told Keith Gordon of *Metro*, "We've been on a world tour. 1989 was our best year ever, our most successful year as far as album sales and attendance. We did a major tour of England, Australia, New Zealand. We did a sold-out tour of Germany, filling 6,000-seat halls. We have a new bass player in the band. Now, Dee Dee is gone and CJ is his replacement, and the band has never been stronger or more exciting than it is now. Things are a lot more pleasant in the band. Now that Dee Dee's gone, we're all getting along great. At one point there was a bit of hostility and that really doesn't exist anymore."

"I think CJ's biggest asset was that he was really strong and tough physically," asserts Rey. "Some of the band was sort of sickly and whatever, so he really pumped some fire into the band. Dee Dee, near the end, was not always 100 percent. And between Joey being sick and Dee Dee being out of it sometimes, CJ made Johnny feel very comfortable because he was so strong on the bass. And he was physically strong. He could do a tour on two hours sleep and be fine the next day. And he worked incredibly cheap too."

"I know that what I did on stage was a throwback to them in the early days," laughs CJ, telling me. "And there's no way I could help that, because I was so influenced by them. I wasn't up there trying to be Dee Dee or trying to mimic anybody. But when Johnny and Joey saw me jumping around—and I know this because I heard them say it—when we were all on stage together, they looked at me and they were like, oh, I better get my ass moving here. They didn't want to get outshined, I guess. No, that's a joke. But it was necessary for them to start moving around more. And they were just excited to be doing it again. They hadn't been touring much because of problems with Dee Dee, Joey, and just problems in general. And they hadn't been excited about anything in a long time. I think there was a bit of nervousness on how the fans were going to actually take it. When I heard Dee Dee quit, I said, 'I'm never going to go to another Ramones show.' And I'm sure there are plenty of other fans who felt the same way."

"When I went to see them, I didn't know what to expect," chuckled Tommy. "They'd replaced Dee Dee and I wondered, 'What am I gonna see here?' And CJ was doing Dee Dee! But a young Dee Dee. I actually got a kick out of it . . . because actually he made the band younger. He took ten years off of them, just by his energy. He was just so excited to be in the band. So I was very pleasantly surprised. . . . They lucked out with CJ."

"*Mondo Bizarro* is a kind of a comeback record," figures CJ. "I would equate it to *Too Tough to Die*. When Tommy stopped working with them, when they did *End of the Century*, to me they had a difficult transition there, because the next great record after *Road to Ruin* is *Too Tough to Die*. And the only difference is that Ed Stasium

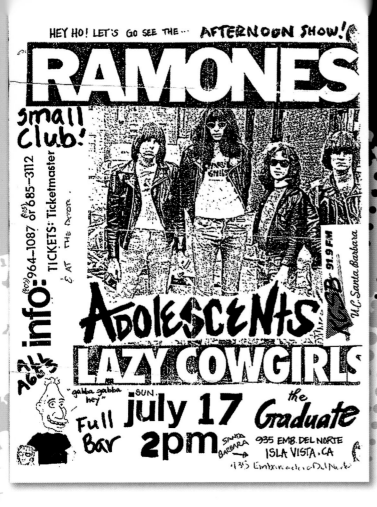

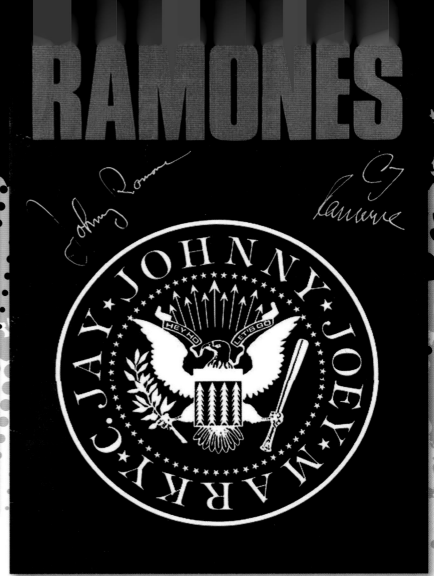

and Tommy came back. Then they got back on that wave of mediocrity—I almost hate to say it. But *Mondo Bizarro* is a second comeback record for them. They staked their place— hey, this is a new point now in our career—and everyone was really excited about it. And Dee Dee wrote some great songs on it and Joey's got a couple good ones, and so I think in the history, it's a pretty important record. Ed's such a humble guy, and you'll never hear him say it or anything, but he really had a lot to do with their sound. I was completely honored to work with him, although I wanted *Mondo Bizarro* to be a little bit more raw, and Ed's style is just not like that."

"I thought *Mondo Bizarro* was a great record," affirms Andy Shernoff. "I think Johnny picked it as one of his least favorites—because there's too many Joey songs on it." Says Andy laughing. "But with Ed Stasium back, it's one of

the better records in the final period of the band's recording history. As far as I'm concerned, the first four Ramones records—each one is a greatest-hits record. Every song on those records is a hit single in a perfect world. And then they made that turn with Phil Spector, and I understand why they did it. And then after that every record has two, three, four, really good songs and then some filler. But *Mondo Bizarro* had some of the better songs in that later period."

Despite the blip in enthusiasm generated by *Mondo Bizarro* in the fans and critics, Rey leans towards a tempered perspective similar to Andy's. "Yes, well, the first four records are genius. Nothing bad about them in any way, shape, or form. So to me, they just blend into one massive four-record set of beautiful music. Some of the recording techniques changed a bit, got a little more

ABOVE LEFT: Still (sigh) playing the "small clubs;" a bill for an afternoon show at a University of California, Santa Barbara campus bar in 1988.

ABOVE RIGHT: Tour program signed by Johnny and CJ, who goes by the rarely seen "C. Jay" in the cover crest.

ABOVE: Catching a bite
at the Hard Rock
Café in New York
City.

RIGHT: Tour laminate
for the *Mondo
Bizarro* campaign;
typically the
higher-level
laminates are
printed in the
hundreds, while
the more widely
distributed "satins"
can be produced in
the thousands.

sophisticated, but they're still
basically the same. From that point
on, there were always a couple of
great songs and great moments on
every record, and there tended to
be a little bit of filler on all the
records—including the ones I was
involved in. When you're on your
fifteenth, sixteenth, seventeenth
album, it's hard to have that same,
oh, I'd like to make every song a
classic. It's more like, let's get a
bunch of great songs, and we'll use
filler for the rest of it. At that
point, the Ramones, no matter what
they did, they'd always sell about
80,000 to 100,000 records. So Johnny
sort of felt like it didn't matter.
Let's get a single so MTV can play
it or radio can play it, even though
they're not going to, and we'll have
a couple of new songs for the set and
we'll just move the machine forward.
What else can you do?"

RAMONES MONDO BIZARRO ALL ACCESS

JOHNNY • JOEY • MARKY • C.JAY

1986—1992 | **157**

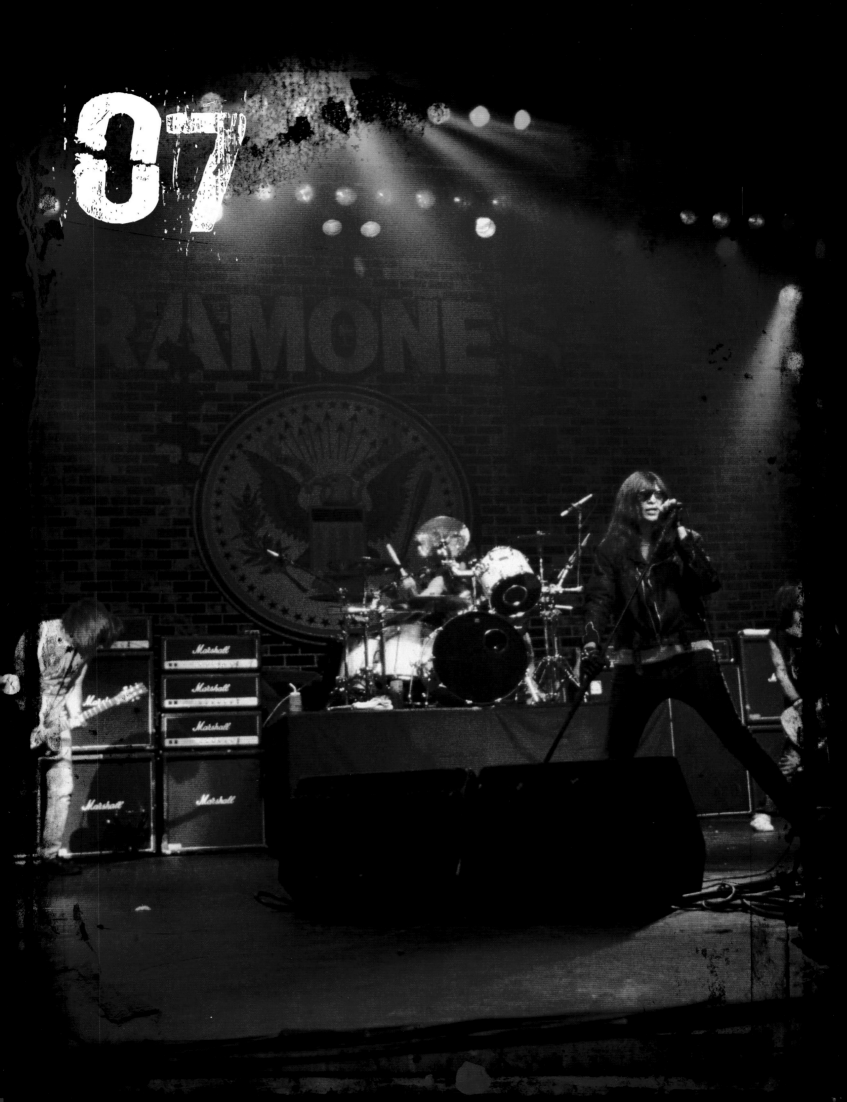

1993–
1994

COVER ME

COVER ME

The Ramones had long been resigned to the fact that manager Gary Kurfirst was not grooming the band for world domination. Having severed ties, amicably, with Seymour Stein and Sire, they were now on Gary's boutique imprint, Radioactive, with the first product of the union, *Mondo Bizarro*, stalling at Number 190 on the *Billboard* chart. Positively distracted by recent tour victories as far away as Japan, Australia, and Argentina, it soon became time to deliver another record to Radioactive, the plan being nothing more than a covers EP, which was eventually to grow into a full-length album. It wasn't that anybody was expecting a Ramones covers album to go gold, but it wasn't out of the question that a wildcard hit single could have fallen out of such a large number of classic rock radio chestnuts redone at one time. Then again, this is the Ramones.

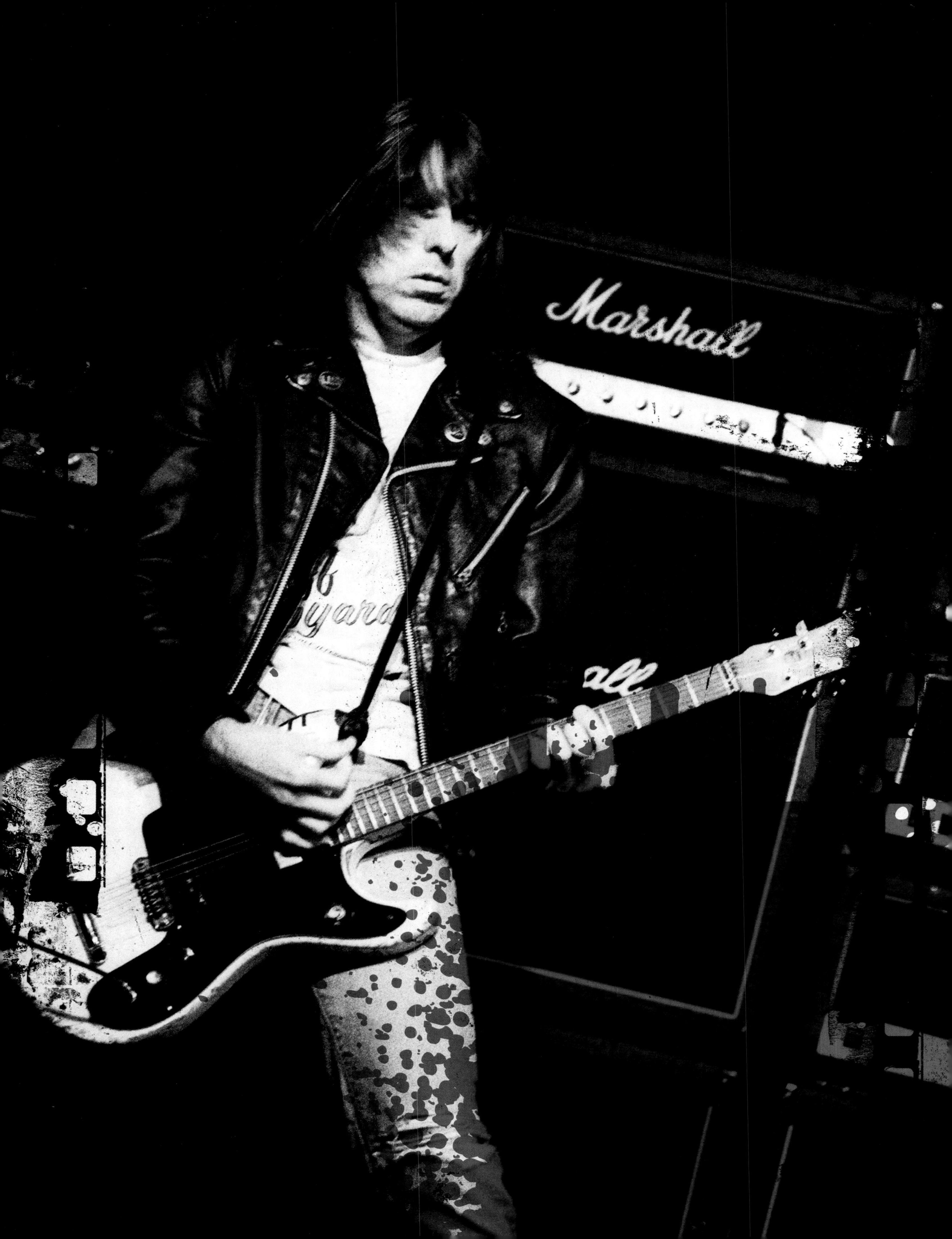
Marshall

ABOVE: Yet another bill with a band harsher, more political, and thornier of disposition than the Ramones ever pretended to be. This one was for the Astoria Theatre, London, in 1995.

"Money," laughs CJ, when asked how the album *Acid Eaters* expanded toward its final twelve-track totality. "Money changed it. There was a bigger advance for it. That's what it was. For the full record, they were going to give us a bigger advance. And that's why you have a lot of filler songs on there. It would've been a strong EP, but to me it was kind of a weak full-length record. I hate to say, but I sing the best songs on it: 'My Back Pages' and 'Journey to the Center of the Mind'——those two are my favorites on the record. I actually like 'Can't Seem to Make You Mine' as well; I like the way Joey sings it. There are probably six or seven strong songs, but like I say, a lot of it is filler. The saddest thing about it is that we had some pretty big musical guests on it, but they are on the weaker tracks, 'Substitute' being one."

"I think Joey reached out to him to sing on it," begins producer of the album Scott Hackwith, when we discuss the band's collaboration on the track with none other than Pete Townshend.

"He was in town for the Broadway premiere of *Tommy*, I believe, so the timing was right. Pete Townshend was one of the reasons I picked up the guitar, and especially having Joey and the Ramones in the room as well, it was fantastic for me. But that day, the president of the label and Gary Kurfirst, and I think Pete's management, all came down to the session. So they're all sitting in the control room, and at that point, I had only produced maybe three or four albums, two of them being my own. So Pete walks in, and I have to sort of tell him what we want him to do, which are the backups on the chorus part. And he was just really silent and didn't say anything. So it was really awkward and all eyes were on me. So he went in and did the part pretty quick. But when he came out, he sat down and talked to me for like a good hour! He was just really warm and really opened up, talking about the studio he was building and stuff. So it started out really uncomfortable, into where it was just really nice to talk with him."

"That record was about keeping
things raw and not getting too crazy
with production," continues Hackwith.
"Just letting them do their version of
the songs with me capturing it. Joey
was such a pro, very particular about
his vocal takes and doing several
vocal takes, and comping together the
best tracks. We were cutting this on
two-inch tape, so we would actually
have to splice tape to do vocal comps,
which got nerve-wracking. Some of
my best times were alone with him.
Afterwards, we would always catch a
cab together to go back to wherever
we were staying. So I had some great
talks with him at like 4 a.m. in the
middle of New York with nobody else
around, which was very surreal. CJ
was a great vocalist too; Joey and
everybody was really behind him doing
that. He was great for the Ramones
at that time. He was like the music
director of the band. He really pulled
things together, the nuts and bolts,
and he held together the rehearsals."

"Marky uses some of the biggest
drumsticks I've ever seen in my life,"

laughs Scott. "He hit the shit out of
the drums. When I first met him, he was
trying to sell me some knives he had
picked up in Venezuela or something—
that was my first impression. But all
my interactions with those guys were
great. It was fun for them because
it's songs that influenced them, plus
there's less stress because they don't
have to worry about writing."

The overall vibe of the record is
energetic and noisy, a sonic quality
that radicalizes, or at least punks
up, songs that might not normally get
such treatment, such as "Have You Ever
Seen the Rain?," "The Shape of Things
to Come," "Surf City," and "I Can't
Control Myself." Most peaceful on
the record is "Out of Time," with a
questionable vocal performance from
Joey, and "When I Was Young"—the
latter was a moderate creative
success, given its creepy psychedelic
treatment. "Had it not been for Scott
really working that record as hard as
he did, those weak songs would've been
a heck of a lot weaker," figures CJ
when we discuss it. "I know he wrung

POLITICAL ANIMAL BOY

JOHNNY RAMONE

One curious subplot of the Ramones' career was Johnny's outspoken Republicanism and support of capitalism, even if he'd allow the left-leaning views of Dee Dee and Joey to sneak through into the band's lyrics more than occasionally.

As he explained to *Spin* in 2001, his philosophy of self-sufficiency and libertarianism started early. "I was always very pro-America, since I was twelve years old. I went to military school and wanted to go into the army and become a general. I hated hippies—hated them. But I always tried to keep politics out of it, because punks weren't supposed to be political; hippies were political. I excused the Clash because they were a great band and they were English."

True to form, the Ramones voiced little about politics that wasn't in a joking or mildly shocking manner, at least up until *Too Tough to Die*, and then, actually, fairly regularly up until the end. Joey and Dee Dee tended to take the podium more often, with CJ getting into the act as well, especially with the pro-gun "Scattergun." As well, Dee Dee would align with Johnny as often as not, a good example being "Punishment Fits the Crime."

"I'm not saying Johnny didn't have those views, but I also think he got great pleasure out of shocking the liberal rock 'n' roll establishment, so to speak," reflects Roberta Bayley. "Like the most shocking thing you could say at the Rock and Roll Hall of Fame is 'God bless President Bush,'" she laughs, "which was almost outrageous, right? In fact, the band's last show

★★★★★
FINAL   **DAILY NEWS**   **15¢**
NEW YORK'S PICTURE NEWSPAPER®
Vol. 56. No. 39   New York, N.Y. 10017, Friday, August 9, 1974*   WEATHER: Partly cloudy, windy and mild.

NIXON RESIGNS

Acts in 'Interest of Nation,' Asks for End to Bitterness

Ford Will Take Oath at Noon, Kissinger Agrees to Stay On

Special 8-Page Pullout; Stories Start on Page 2

at CBGB was when they played a benefit for the cops to get bulletproof vests. Now that seems like a normal thing to do, but then it felt a little weird. To me, that seems like a nice, sensible thing to do. The cops had a dangerous job in New York, and people—well, white people anyway—had a pretty good relationship with them at that time. The city was so dangerous and in so much turmoil that you didn't want to be the enemy of the cops. But at the time it seemed like a pretty non-liberal thing to be doing, to raise money for bulletproof vests. It was a bit controversial because from the hippie era you were supposed to be anti-cop, and so pro-cop was a new idea."

ABOVE: August 9, 1974. Nixon resigns, four months after the birth of the Ramones, who were soon to get their own presidential seal courtesy of Arturo Vega.

Marky takes a typically dim and laconic Queens' boy view of the situation, and remembers being a little extra fed-up because politics turned out to be yet another impediment to Joey and Johnny getting along: "Johnny liked Ronald Reagan and Joey liked whoever was running on the Democratic ticket. When Nixon resigned and later was pardoned by Gerald Ford who was vice president at the time, Johnny felt that shouldn't have happened, that in fact he should have stayed president. But he got caught, and that's what happens. So I guess Nixon did the right thing in resigning. Then Joey would go, like, 'I told you so,'

stuff like that. But in the end, music is what matters. And when you're in a van fifteen years—I did 1,700 shows with the group—there's bound to be some confrontation. But with the politics, it was mainly Joey and Johnny. Joey was a liberal and Johnny was a right-wing conservative. The verbal confrontations would be along the lines of, 'Why did you vote for him?' 'Why are you a conservative?' 'Why do you like rock music?' 'There's no room for that in the rock world.' There were a lot of petty animosities when it came to arguing about politics. But these guys had no in-depth knowledge. Half the time they didn't know what they were talking about."

"WE GREW UP IN THE '60S AND WE'VE BEEN BIG FANS AND RECORD COLLECTORS OF THE BEST THINGS THAT HAVE GONE DOWN. NOWADAYS, THE RECORD BUSINESS IS A REAL BUSINESS AND EVERYTHING THAT'S COMING OUT IS REAL STERILE, REAL SAFE AND VERY BUSINESS-ORIENTED. . . . THERE'S NO INDIVIDUALISM IN MUSIC TODAY, WHERE ROCK 'N' ROLL USED TO BE REBELLIOUS. IT USED TO BE UNIQUE. THERE'S A MINORITY OF PEOPLE WHO DO CARE ABOUT MUSIC, AND WE'RE THE MINORITY. IT'S THE INDIVIDUAL WHO'S GOING TO KEEP ROCK 'N' ROLL ALIVE."

JOEY RAMONE

LEFT: Simple yet classy T-shirt art commemorating the covers album.

every little bit of energy he could possibly get out of them."

Spicing up proceedings were guest appearances from Traci Lords (who was also managed by Kurfirst) on "Somebody to Love" and Sebastian Bach on "Out of Time"—the Skid Row front man showing up all high-fives with a whiskey bottle, and quickly winning over a dubious Hackwith with his enthusiasm for singing and his ability to work out "crazy harmonies."

"I want to say the whole process took six months, from start to finish," reflects Hackwith. "Yeah, at first it was a couple months, doing tracking, at Chung King, which was a great studio—a lot of hip-hop records were produced in that studio. Great gear, great space, good vibe, smaller room than I'm used to on the West Coast, but great equipment. And then I ended up going for a couple more months when

they decided to do a full album, and then there was the mixing process."

"We always loved '60s bands, the older bands," Marky comments in closing, on the fact that *Acid Eaters* at least shows some cohesiveness around era, if not specific styles within that era. "We always liked the Phil Spector sound, the surf sound, original rock, and we figured, let's do songs we always liked. I picked seven out of those songs, but there were two I wanted to do that John wasn't able to play guitar on: 'Kicks' by Paul Revere and the Raiders and 'Incense and Peppermints' by the Strawberry Alarm Clock, because it was called *Acid Eaters*, and it was an ode to the psychedelic era. So if those two were included, that album would've been a ten out of ten, although the production could have been better."

CRUMMY STUFF

Record labels often loosen the purse strings and order up some sort of promo item to send out with their charge's latest album, the idea being that an additional token of appreciation would prompt print coverage or radio spins, or at least sit on a shelf and remind that media person that the band exists. Here's a survey of some sweet Ramones items, as picked (and commented on) by Ramones scholar and collector Jari-Pekka Laitio-Ramone.

1) LETTER OPENER/POCKET KNIFE

Sent to select press with *Leave Home*. "This rare item shows up on ebay maybe once every two years."

2) BLACK BASEBALL BAT, CIRCA *RAMONES*

"There are three different mini-sized (16-inch) black baseball bats sent by Sire. The first one (shown here on opposite page) says 'THE RAMONES — A HIT ON SIRE RECORDS,' and a second says 'BLITZKRIEG BOP. THE RAMONES — A HIT ON SIRE RECORDS.' There's a third UK version which focuses on 'Beat on the Brat' instead of 'Blitzkrieg Bop.' Later on, Sire Records ordered a different kind of promotional baseball bat, from the Hillerich & Bradsby Company, who produced the Ramones model of the famous Louisville Slugger® bat. The Ramones model is thirty-one inches long."

3) PLASTIC BOX OF PINS SENT WITH *ROAD TO RUIN* AND/OR THE "NEEDLES AND PINS" SINGLE

"Both boxes are clear except that they have printed in the white parts of the *Road to Ruin* drawings, the Sire Records logo and a bit of additional text."

4) *¡ADIOS AMIGOS!* BOTTLE OF TEQUILA WITH SHOT GLASS

"It's a real miniature bottle of tequila complete with worm inside the bottle, Ramones logo and dinosaur illustration. I still haven't opened mine."

4

5) *MONDO BIZARRO* LEATHER JACKETS

"Radioactive Records sent these with the album. There were also badges in a few variants."

6) *TALKIN' MONDO BIZARRO* PROMOTIONAL CD

"This radio promo includes a twenty-six-minute-long interview with Joey about the album and the history of band. There are also four songs from *Mondo Bizarro* recorded live at the Hollywood Palladium in Los Angeles."

7) "CRUMMY STUFF" PROMO PACKAGE OF COOKIES

"A circular package of cookies was sent, at least in Switzerland, in a red-and-white package. Only a few of these rolls of cookies have survived."

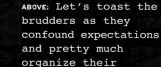

ABOVE: Let's toast the brudders as they confound expectations and pretty much organize their exit—salut!

3

2

8

ABOVE: The famous bat, from a band that frankly eschewed and avoided violence, except in the abstract, placed in front of a signed Ramones poster, sadly missing Joey's signature. Above that, the highly nifty "Needles & Pins" promo piece.

8) PROMOTIONAL PHOTOS

"There are of course a lot of these. One of the rarest is of Joey and Richie Stotts of the Plasmatics, which was taken by Clark Krueger in 1984 after Joey and Stotts did a demo of the song, 'Rock and Roll Is the Answer.' It took twenty-eight years to get the song issued. Stotts told me in 2006, 'I may have played the song a couple of times with my band in 1984–85, but I had completely forgotten about the tape actually until a friend of mine was over at my house in 2002/03, and we were looking through some of my older stuff that I could put out. I found that tape I made with Joey and made a call to Joe Blaney, the producer.' 'Rock and Roll Is the Answer' was available

as a limited edition 7-inch on Record Store Day, April 21, 2012, and it was the first single from Joey's second solo album, . . . *Ya Know?.*"

9) *BRAIN DRAIN* WRISTWATCH

"This UK-only item reads, 'Ramones drain the UK 1989.'"

10) *ROCK WERCHTER* PUZZLE GAME

"*Rock Werchter* is an annual Belgian music festival held in the village of Werchter since 1976. Its 1985 lineup included the Ramones, U2, REM, Depeche Mode, Paul Young, Joe Cocker, Lloyd Cole, and the Style Council. One promo item was this kind of puzzle game printed with the names of the artists."

08

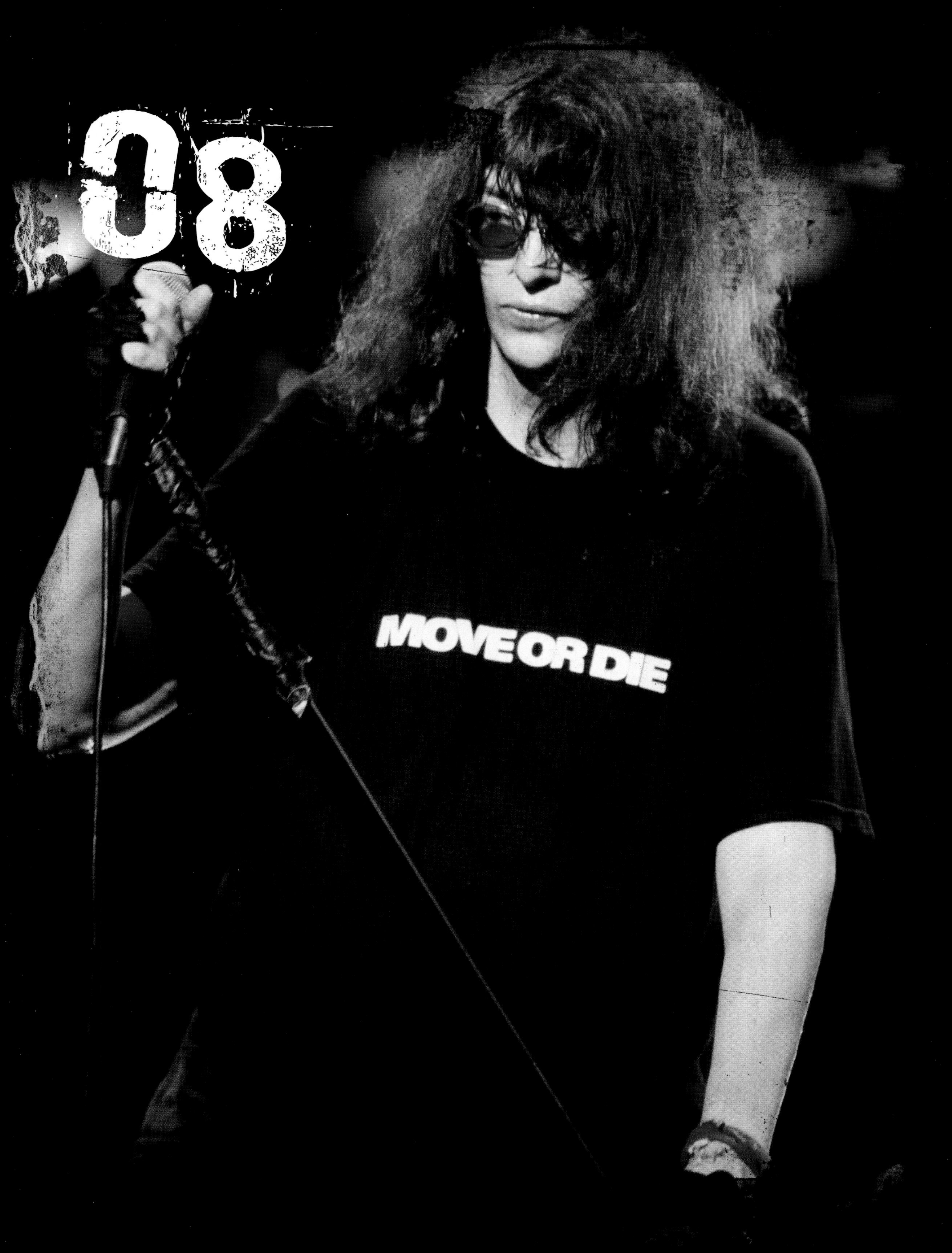

1995...
1996

"IT WASN'T LIKE IT WAS
GOING TO KILL HIM..."

"IT WASN'T LIKE IT WAS GOING TO KILL HIM. . . ."

Typical of his provocative and negative nature, Johnny had been daydreaming out loud and in public about retirement at least back to *End of the Century* times, with the declarations becoming more realistic and concrete at the beginning of the *Acid Eaters* album cycle. As it turned out, putting the Ramones to rest would become a textbook example of how to end a band, even if parts of the orchestration didn't go to plan.

In truth, the historical neatness of the retirement was in all likelihood aided and ensured by the actions of the Grim Reaper, who would mercilessly and repeatedly visit the band before they could think about reunion tours, one more album, compromised lineups trading on their goodly name, more live albums, shot vocals, and dwindling crowds grumbling about their diminishing powers. Instead, the Ramones voiced their goodbyes right on the front of their last record cover, and then ground it out on the road until Joey was fit to drop.

Hamburg, 1996. Roberta Bayley on the band's visual presentation live: "There are some early pictures of Johnny in silver lamé pants; in the very early days, there was a little more flexibility in their look. But very, very quickly it became really rigid and almost like a uniform. And yes, they dressed off the stage pretty much as they did on the stage. But then they brought it to this intensity on stage, where they would all come on with their leather jackets, and they would take them off at a certain point in the set. Pretty quickly they locked into that look."

"In '94, me and Johnny and Joey sat in a hotel room, and we discussed our retirement, which came two years later, in '96," explains Marky to me. "But we had to do two more years of touring, and do our last shows. You don't just do a last show and that's it. You've got to do your last show all over the world, which is what we had to do. So that's how that came about. It was time, and we left on a high note, and that was the result."

It was within this framework that the band went back to Baby Monster Studios in New York (home of *Mondo Bizarro*) with Daniel Rey in the first couple months of 1995, to slam out another Ramones album at home on the cheap and raw, so that they could hit the road, heads held high, with new material.

"They liked it to be New York so they could sleep at home," laughs Rey in our interview. "They liked it to be cheap so they wouldn't spend all their advance. And that was it, really. Joey would sing at night, and the band would cut in the daytime; that's usually how it went. Baby Monster was a great studio on 14th Street that the band liked a lot. Very close to where they lived, good price, great equipment, low-key vibe, and Joey liked it and felt comfortable there. The budget was usually about $125,000 on these records, give or take a few thousand. And they'd cut the records for $50,000 or $60,000, and they'd split up the rest."

"Not a lot of synthesizers or drum machines," answers Rey, when asked about the complexion of his production job on the album. "They wanted to make a simple album that represented the Ramones live. We wanted to make it bare-bones and raw."

As for what is at the core of the band's sound, Joey in a *Live Wire* 1995 interview offers, surprisingly and graciously, "Johnny's guitar sound—it's become the most imitated sound these days. We just have a particular style and way of looking at things. It sounds simple, but it's really very complex! We never change; we only get better. We've maintained

a distinct sound and style. I don't think that there has been a style that has taken hold since the Ramones. Before there was Led Zeppelin, the Beatles and the Stones—they all have a distinct style—and then there was us."

In the months leading up to recording the album, and after a live campaign with the Brazilian heavy metal band Sepultura that underscored the Ramones' immense following in South America, Joey returned home to a grim diagnosis: lymphoma.

"I'm not really sure of the dates, but he wasn't particularly sick when I found out," says Rey. "He was getting ready to begin treatments and stuff. But it didn't really come up too much during *¡Adios Amigos!*. He didn't really let on. He was somewhat in denial and didn't want to talk about it. Because it wasn't really showing up, you know what I mean? He was diagnosed with it,

but he wasn't suffering from it. So he probably figured that if it wasn't there, [he didn't] want to talk about it or bring it up."

"It didn't seem like it was life-threatening," says Andy Shernoff, who was confided in immediately, and would be at the bedside when Joey died. "But he didn't want the band to know his personal business, so he didn't tell them. I never thought it was going to kill him, because I thought it was like a lower grade. You hear about people surviving this. I was concerned, but it wasn't like it was going to kill him."

The highlight on the band's final album, *¡Adios Amigos!*, was far and away the opening track, "I Don't Want to Grow Up." It was not written by the band but by Tom Waits and Kathleen Brennan, with prescient lyrics (continued on page 180)

OPPOSITE: In Brazil, the Ramones were of a stature big enough to get near equal billing with home-grown heroes made good, Sepultura. "Any Latin country that you go to [knows the Ramones]," qualifies CJ Ramone. "I know in Brazil they speak Portuguese, but Argentina, Uruguay, Paraguay, even Central America and Spain—you go to those places, all the street kids, they all love the Ramones. It's an intense thing to see. The first time I went over there, I could not believe how crazy the kids went."

ADIOS AMIGOS

RAMONES

HEY HO   LET'S GO

THE FINAL TOUR

Jan 19 – Budrio, Italy
Jan 20 – Pordenone, Italy
Jan 22 – Milan, Italy
Jan 23 – Munich, Germany
Jan 24 – Offenbach, Germany
Jan 26 – Bonn, Germany
Jan 28 – Berlin, Germany
Jan 29 – Hamburg, Germany
Jan 30 – Hannover, Germany
Jan 31 – Amsterdam, Netherlands
Feb 2 – Kortrijk, Belgium
Feb 3 – London, England
Feb 12 – Providence, RI
Feb 13 – Northampton, MA
Feb 14 – Boston, MA
Feb 16 – Philadelphia, PA
Feb 17 – Washington, DC
Feb 18 – Port Chester, NY
Feb 20 – Harrisburg, PA
Feb 21 – Lido Beach, NY
Feb 23 – New Haven, CT

Feb 24 – Baltimore, MD
Feb 25 – Red Bank, NJ
Feb 27, 28, 29 – New York, NY
Mar 7 – Rio De Janeiro, Brazil
Mar 8 – Moogi, Brazil
Mar 10 – Santo Andre, Brazil
Mar 11, 12, 13 – São Paulo, Brazil
Mar 15 – Buenos Aires, Argentina
Apr 18 – Indianapolis, IN
Apr 19 – Chicago, IL
Apr 20 – Kalamazoo, MI
Apr 21 – Detroit, MI
Apr 23 – Cleveland, OH
Apr 25 – Allentown, PA
Apr 26 – Pittsburgh, PA
Apr 27 – Rochester, NY
Apr 28 – Albany, NY
Apr 30 – New York, NY
May 1 – New York, NY
May 22 – Little Rock, AR
May 23 – Memphis, TN

May 25 – Atlanta, GA
May 26 – Birmingham, AL
June 27 – Kansas City, MO
June 28 – Des Moines, IA
July 2 – Indianapolis, IN
July 3 – Buckeye Lake, OH
July 5 – Barrie, Canada
July 7 – Quebec City, Canada
July 9 – Pownal, VT
July 10, 11 – New York, NY
July 13 – Syracuse, NY
July 16 – Charles Town, WV
July 18 – West Palm Beach, FL
July 20 – Rockingham, NC
July 21 – Newport, TN
July 23 – New Orleans, LA
July 25 – Ferris, TX
July 27 – Phoenix, AZ
July 30 – George, WA
Aug 2 – San Jose, CA
Aug 3, 4 – Irvine, CA
Aug 6 – Los Angeles, CA –
The Last Show.

GLOBAL A GO-GO

THE RAMONES AS WORLD CITIZENS

There's no denying that the Ramones can be called a global phenomenon. This is a fuzzy conceit, and one that frankly can be claimed by bigger bands on a bigger scale and through more territories. Still, the Ramones are an interesting case, in that what they represent abroad is necessarily tied to their unique and cartoony caricature, one that incorporates dress, music, lyrics, and graphic design, much of it shot through with signifiers of the USA and of original rock 'n' roll from the '50s.

"Yes, they do belong to the world," agrees punk expert Ralph Alfonso. "The Ramones are in that category. See, one of the reasons Europeans have a bit of a hate on sometimes for Americans is that Americans sometimes don't know their own culture. They don't know what they have, right? So first time to France, I'm walking around, what the hell is going on? James Dean and Marilyn Monroe are everywhere. You go into the record shops, and there's Gene Vincent, Eddie Cochran, MC5. And you go back to Canada and the States, and good luck finding any of that stuff. But in Europe, once they see you're a music guy, it's, 'Oh, what do you know about Iggy?' The Ramones represent that kind of Americana ideal. The Ramones translate everywhere. The music is so primal and simplistic and so are the lyrics. That's the key: if you have really simple lyrics, everybody around the world can kind of understand it."

The first thing that comes to mind for Roberta Bayley is the lyrics: "Yes, I think that's why they resonated in so many different countries. It was a strong and simple message that the kids could grasp, without having to necessarily know the words; it didn't really need translation. Also, Dee Dee was raised partly in Germany and they have this crazy mix of Johnny with his whole right-wing thing, and Joey being very Jewish, and then we find out later that Tommy was also Jewish."

It's a good point, and not so much because Dee Dee grew up in Germany, but Germany is referenced periodically in the lyrics (Nazi or otherwise), as is Havana, and various American locales. The band also toured Europe extensively as well as Japan, and then, arriving late, found their boldest base in South America, with Argentina in particular being crazy for the Ramones, followed by Brazil.

Then there's the fact that Arturo is Hispanic, with his view on the mania being that Latin American fans appreciate the nihilism and hopelessness of punk in general. Arturo's "presidential seal" logo for the band would have also helped, given that many foreign rock fans like large doses of Americana in their American bands, one example being the strong showing for southern rock in France. The almost governmental logo aside, the Ramones are viewed as goofy rock ambassadors of the world's favorite metropolis, New York City, by near consensus capital of the world and a beloved and magical place for 50 million tourists a year.

Finally, the Ramones closed shop on a sour note when Joey passed on a million-dollar deal to play one last time in South America, which would have been a fitting end for the band, in front of their most enduring fans. Such was the ultimate gesture, unconsummated, that proved where loyalties for this band with no gold records really resided.

"By far the band's biggest audiences would be in South America," figures Flo Hayler, who also puts into practice the global nature of the band through

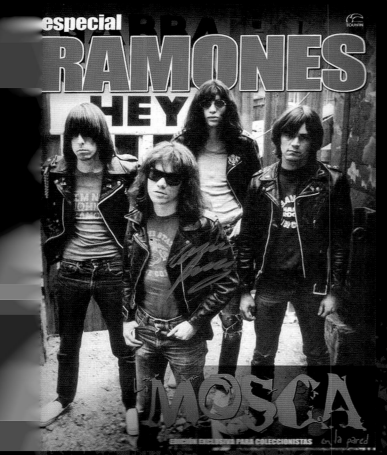

became
y commonplace
the Ramones
rs of foreign
e magazines—
wn by a 2004
edition of
Mosca magazine
nd 2004
rs edition,
with poster,
lian *Coleçao*
. After
ey, Johnny,
, and Tommy
nted all
magically
n in the
st sense,
rough their
60s, '70s,
n '80s
ngs, across
essive number
generations.

The inimitable
mone in 1991.

his classy Ramones Museum in Berlin. "The Ramones are a religion down there—because it's easy to join the gang. In South America, everybody looks like a Ramone. The Japanese have the same thing. I was in Japan with CJ Ramone recently, and I saw kids that look exactly like Dee Dee Ramone or Johnny Ramone—exactly."

"Well, I do know that the Latin countries love us, including Spain and Mexico," adds Richie Ramone, "but why, I don't know. They really love their rock 'n' roll there; they're not inhibited. They come out and they come up big and kick it; they're ready to party with you. They're not afraid to jump up and down, and smash things around. They like to have a good time and they're my favorite audiences around the world."

"A major fact has to be the band's imagery," notes Ralph Alfonso, adding a final few nuances to the question of the band's appeal abroad. "Which doesn't change and is iconic. It's this idealization of an America that doesn't really exist. But it's an

to exist, right? Everybody wants the James Dean walking down [a] New York street thing. Everybody wants Gene Vincent in leather. To the point where Europeans, when they have American bands from the '50s or '60s come over, part of the deal is, they'll go, 'We're going to fly you over, but here's the set list we want you to play. If your band can't do it, then we'll get our players.' And the Ramones slotted perfectly into that ethos, because they never changed, and you're going to get all the hits and more. Joey is Joey, and Johnny's got all the poses down and is going to do what Johnny does. The Ramones are not going to let you down."

"Had they lived," sums up Lenny Kaye, "the Ramones would arguably, today, be more successful in Japan, or Brazil, or Europe than any of their peers, because their music translates so easily. In breaking down the building blocks of rock to its most simplistic form, they translated all over the world really easily. And so I think their muse and their music is

"THEY COULD NEVER FIND A MOLD FOR US. WE HAVE A DEFINITE VISION, AN ATTITUDE AND HONEST ALTHOUGH IT HURTS YOU IN A LOT OF WAYS, AS A BAND, YOU END UP FEELING GOOD ABOUT WHAT YOU'VE DONE. YOU'RE DOING IT FOR YOURSELF AND YOUR FANS, WH APPRECIATE YOU BEING SINCERE. WE TURNED THE WORLD AROUND TO A NEW SOUND, A NEW ATTITUDE. WE PUT THE EXCITEMENT BACK INT ROCK 'N' ROLL, MADE IT WHAT IT WAS ALWAYS MEANT TO BE."

so poignantly delivered by Joey, much like his later solo rendition of "It's a Wonderful World."

"When we did *Acid Eaters*, I wanted to do that [Tom Waits] song," explains CJ. "I wanted to put that song on the record and it didn't happen. Joey was also a big Tom Waits fan, and so when we went into the studio to do the last one, I was like, 'Joey, we gotta get this song on the record. I already figured it out, I know how it's going to sound, we can do a really good version of this.' And I said, 'It fits perfectly with the Ramones' whole thing—the eternal teenagers.' Joey was like, alright, I'll submit it, and this way it will definitely get on. Because if I submitted it, Johnny would've shot it down and it wouldn't have made it. So Joey submitted it and I seconded it. And then once Johnny heard it, he agreed that it was a good take. I've been a Tom Waits fan for a long time; nobody else does what he does. Of course, in turn, Tom covered 'The Return of Jackie and Judy' and

he also recorded 'Danny Says.' But disagreeing with Johnny was always a pointless endeavor, which is what 'Got Alot to Say' is about—it's typical of how I was when I was in the band. I would try to get my point across to him but it just never worked out great."

So, like everybody else, CJ had to read carefully the dynamic between Johnny and Joey; still, he had an advantage. "Keeping in mind that I got into the Ramones, right out of the Marine Corps, Johnny was the perfect boss for me," explains CJ to me. "Because he did not ever mince words or leave any gray area. He always told you exactly what he expected, exactly what he wanted. And that was perfect for me. I had no problems with people yelling in my face. I could take orders, which had a lot to with why Johnny chose me. Johnny went to military school as a kid, so he learned his leadership qualities in the same way that I learned to take orders, pretty much. So it was a very easy pairing."

ABOVE: Who's that metal guy? Well, it's CJ Ramone, of course . . . "I mostly came from a heavy metal background—my favorite band was Black Sabbath. I always liked punk, but the problem is that I lived in a blue-collar town, and nobody where I lived liked punk rock—everybody was into metal. But I'm lucky enough that my dad, who of course I got most of my music from, was always was into good music. And that's how and why I shared some of the influences that the Ramones had— especially the '50s stuff." Band shot is from the MTV Movie Awards in Los Angeles, California, 1995.

"Johnny ran a very tight ship, but this is the thing that everybody forgets," continues CJ. "Johnny was the way he was because he had to be. You look at who he's dealing with in the band. You had Dee Dee who is the crazy genius rock 'n' roll songwriter, but had problems with substance abuse and alcohol abuse and could not organize himself for the most part. You had Joey who is Joey, suffers badly with OCD, another guy who couldn't organize himself pretty much. . . . And then Mark went through a whole bunch of stuff himself, with substances. So, Johnny was the one holding the whole thing together. If Johnny wasn't in the band, the Ramones would've split up years before, long before they ever did anything. It takes that type of person, and that's how I saw Johnny's role. To give an example, we had an argument one time. Joey was really sick. I told Joey, you know, why don't you just take some time off? And Johnny came to me the next day and he was like, 'Just keep your mouth shut. Do your job. You

don't know what's going on. You have no idea what's going on.' And when Johnny first said it, I was not real happy with him. But after a while, I began to see what he was talking about, and he was absolutely right. Joey would take time off, and then he would go and work on all these other projects and travel and do all this stuff, instead of staying home and taking care of himself like he said he was going to. And that really bothered Johnny, and that's why he put the brakes on taking any time off."

Another major element on the record is the inclusion of five songs written by Dee Dee (now not in the band) with Daniel Rey, the record's producer. Three of these—"Makin' Monsters for My Friends," "The Crusher," and "Cretin Family"—establish a tight punk tone for the record. CJ handled the lead vocal like a smart-mouthed young punk on all three, as well as his on own track, "Scattergun."

"That wasn't my doing; that was Johnny's doing," says Rey in our interview. "It was just easier.

HEY! HO! LET'S GO

"Oh, doing that Cadillac commercial was funny," answers Marky Ramone, when asked about the Ramones' influence on and invasion of pop culture, with "Blitzkrieg Bop" in particular now having been used to sell everything from cola to suntan lotion to cable networks. "They used 'Rock 'n' Roll Radio,' comparing us to all these other people in the commercial, saying that we were geniuses and how we started in a garage, which they didn't—the band started in the basement below [Joey's] mother's art store. It's little things like that that are funny, when you realize that we were who we were, and now we're in a Cadillac commercial, not to mention hearing 'Hey, ho, let's go' at Yankee Stadium."

Indeed "Blitzkrieg Bop" has become a perennial at a wide range of sporting events the world over, with its signature chant insidiously, over time, becoming part of the English-language lexicon as has, to a lesser extent, "Gabba gabba hey!"

Reinforcing the band's place in pop culture are the accolades, ranging from a spot on *The Simpsons* in 1993, the major label *We're a Happy Family* tribute album and *End of the Century* documentary—both in 2003, to a Rock and Roll Hall of Fame induction in 2002, a Grammy Lifetime Achievement Award in 2011, countless magazine poll placements, and the designation of East 2nd and Bowery in New York as Joey Ramone Place, also in 2003. "Rockaway Beach" was even used in a radio campaign to entice tourists back to the northeastern US coast after it was ravaged by Hurricane Sandy.

"Their music has lived on in a way that nobody—especially them—would've been able to predict," reflects Lenny

Kaye. "Somewhere right now, there's somebody playing a Ramones song in a jam session. And everybody can play along with it, because it's so present and there. Their legacy remains, because you can see it in hardcore, but more so you can see it in these kids just learning how to play guitar. It's a great entry into the world of electric music. So by being so elemental, their legend continues on. And no question they have become legends . . . much to the surprise of Johnny Winter fans who bottled them when they opened up for him for their first time outside of New York. They carved out a place for themselves, and the fact that they're not here to enjoy this afterglow of fame is one of the great sadnesses I have about rock 'n' roll from that era. Instead of continually having to fight for their foothold, they deserve to be playing that music all over the world and be respected for it—but of course they can't."

ABOVE: A typically frumpy-looking French 1976 7-inch picture sleeve, pre-haircuts.

OPPOSITE: The Ramones were given a Lifetime Achievement Award Grammy in 2011, proudly displayed here by Marky; it's the type of accolade that attempts to make right on a lifetime of not receiving deserved accolades—from the Grammy folks and otherwise.

CJ could sing, knock it off in a night, where Joey would take a week constantly re-singing, fixing, I want to change this word and this word. That was really the only reason. Most of the time on these records was spent on vocals. Johnny knew that, so CJ sang. And also live, if CJ could sing one or two of them in the set, it could give Joey a break."

As for the contribution from the original punk in the band, explains Rey, "Dee Dee was living in Amsterdam, and I went over there to write and gather some songs for the album, which were good songs, all goofy and fun and comic books. The Ramones paid for me to go there, which was really incredible. It was pragmatic. They needed songs and Dee Dee needed to write, so let's continue the relationship. It's more like Dee Dee just couldn't deal with the drama. In Amsterdam, Dee Dee moved around a lot. Every time I would talk to him, he would be in a different apartment with a different dog and a different guitar. But he was living nicely.

It was great; he looked at himself as a troubadour, traveling, like Woody Guthrie. Plus we got him to lay down a vocal over the phone in fake German, for 'Born to Die in Berlin'——*that is cool*."

"He actually stopped by the studio once when he was in New York," continues Rey. "I think it was the last time they all kind of hung out together. Things were actually pretty good. They weren't really mad at him for leaving anymore, and he wasn't mad. He was happy to be contributing to the record. It was all very nice, and he didn't stay too long—which was also very nice. The guys were happy to see him and happy to have him go."

Joey's contributions to the record, however slight, were also songs of a higher quality, strengthening ¡Adios Amigos!, as did Rey's tough and guitar-y production job. "She Talks to Rainbows" is a moody, darkly melodic song with textural guitars, while "Life's a Gas" serves as a touching goodbye from Joey. It is characteristic of him, with the

> **"BUT THAT'S THE STORY OF THE RAMONES' CAREER—
> AWKWARD. AWKWARD FROM BEGINNING TO END—VERY
> AWKWARD. THEY BECAME POPULAR IN SPITE OF THEIR
> CAREER. IT'S THE STRANGEST THING, REALLY WEIRD. BUT
> HAVING A PERFECT CAREER AND A PERFECT LIFE AND
> EVERYTHING, IT JUST WAS NOT IN THE CARDS FOR A
> MISFIT BAND. IT JUST WASN'T IN THE CARDS FOR THEM."**
> CJ RAMONE

mumbler-in-chief saying his piece in under twenty words, repeated like a classic Ramones' mantra.

"I thought it was a great last album," sums up Marky to me. "Daniel got a great sound for the whole band, for our last hurrah. Don't forget, Daniel played lead guitar on a lot of the albums because Johnny couldn't play lead guitar. In the past we used Walter Lure from Johnny Thunders' the Heartbreakers, but we'd gotten Daniel Rey on board to play lead guitar too. So it's good that he would produce a few albums, because he was also involved with the musicianship."

Less pleased with ¡Adios Amigos! was CJ, who calls it, "more like a last gasp record than anything else. There are some good songs, but it was kind of weak. I really wish I would've had some of my own songs from my own *Bad Chopper* record, or any of the songs

from these last two records I put out, *Reconquista* and *Last Chance to Dance*. I wish I would've had some of the songs on those two records written at the time. I felt as a goodbye record, it just wasn't strong enough. A swan song should be something unbelievable. Even if they would've hired outside songwriters to come in and copy their style and make sure that it was a really great record, even that would've been acceptable to me. But to put out a weak record, I don't know. But that's the story of the Ramones' career—awkward. Awkward from beginning to end—very awkward. They became popular in spite of their career. It's the strangest thing, really weird. But having a perfect career and a perfect life and everything, it just was not in the cards for a misfit band. It just wasn't in the cards for them."

OPPOSITE: The band on August 6, 1996. Despite varying the lineup, the Ramones stayed true to their essence. "We did very well," says Marky, lower left, when asked about the money. "That's because of the constant touring in the last fifteen years. Plus the songs are being played over the radio everywhere, and in commercials— you name it. Merchandise ... we live in a capitalistic society. So all that came, and it did very well for us. In the beginning, the band and the genre weren't accepted that well, so it took a little time."

1997-2014

"ETERNAL TEENAGERS"

"ETERNAL TEENAGERS"

So Johnny had in him one last military campaign, and its scope was to be impressive. Armed with a creditable final album of aggressive melodic punk, boldly recorded, and featuring a brave twist in lots of songs sung by the youth wing of the band—CJ Ramone—the band hit the road. Summer '95 saw the Ramones playing the United States before mounting a six-day stand in Buenos Aires, followed by their most detailed Japanese tour to date. Into 1996, the band played Canada, Europe, more USA dates, and even got back to South America again. It all made sense until it didn't.

"Well, our last tour was Lollapalooza," laughs CJ to me, "so the meaning of that whole final tour thing was just totally lost."

Indeed, after performing a relentless range of dates that could have served as any band's swan song, the Ramones jumped on the noisy traveling circus that was Lollapalooza, dwarfed by the likes of Metallica and Soundgarden, but supported in punk by Rancid—the big neo-punk band of the moment.

"And it was totally lost because we were playing big, huge shows—we weren't the headliner. I'm not saying we didn't get treated good or treated with respect. When Johnny told me that they wanted to do the Lollapalooza tour, I told him no. I said, I told you four years ago I was going on a motorcycle trip. I'm not going to do it. I said, do yourself a favor, call up Dee Dee, call up Tommy, put together the original band, do Lollapalooza, you can bring Marky and me in on a couple of shows, but do Lollapalooza as the original lineup. The fans will love it, the press will love it, it'll be a very poetic end to a really awkward career. I said, just take my advice on this. This would be a really good thing for you guys."

PAGE 188: Johnny rocks out at Lollapalooza, Spartan Stadium August 2, 1996 in San Jose, California.

LOLLAPALOOZA '96
...and much much more!

METALLICA
SOUNDGARDEN
SPECIAL GUESTS
RAMONES
RANCID
THE SHAOLIN KUNGFU OF CHINA
SCREAMING TREES
PSYCHOTICA

SECOND STAGE
Girls Against Boys
Ben Folds Five
Ruby
Cornershop
You Am I
Beth Hart Band

INDIE STAGE
Chune
Moonshake
Lutefisk
Capsize 7

For more info on tickets, special guests and anything else, visit us on the internet at http://lollapalooza.com/

FRIDAY JULY 5 • MOLSON PARK

LEFT: Lollapalooza '96 sensibly and logically bricked punk to metal through the mortar of grunge.

BELOW: The Ramones "finale" for their fans—Lollapalooza, July 1996, at Downing Stadium, Randall's Island, New York City.

DON'T WORRY ABOUT ME

Each of the Ramones, save for Johnny, cranked out creditable solo material after the band locked up shop. Aside from the enigmatic Tommy, who had a bluegrass band called Uncle Monk, much of the material generated was essentially in the Ramones wheelhouse, ranging mostly from fairly loud old-time rock 'n' roll, through pop punk to hardcore and metal.

Dee Dee was the most prolific, with *Zonked!*, from 1997, being a highlight. Marky had his bands, the Intruders and the SpeedKings, but also played on Dee Dee's and Joey's records, plus those of myriad other artists. Richie took his time, but came up with a rock-solid, hard-hitting solo record in 2013 called *Entitled*. For CJ's part, he played with Los Gusanos and Bad Chopper, but also crafted a pair of fine solo albums, *Reconquista*, 2012, and *Last Chance to Dance*—the latter from 2014 arguably the best of the solo bunch.

But most important to the story of the Ramones from the solo end of things—singers and front men usually trump everyone else—is the fact that we got two solo albums out of Joey, both issued posthumously, *Don't Worry About Me* in 2002, followed by . . . *Ya Know?* in 2012.

"Chemo debilitates you," explains Andy Shernoff, who worked with Joey on the songs from both records. "There were two different tracking sessions for the record. He would sing when he could sing, and he sang in Daniel's apartment, which was two or three blocks from Joey's apartment, a very comfortable situation for him. I think the vocal on 'Wonderful World' is as good as any vocal Joey ever did. He was starting to use different aspects of his voice, different colors. It's

one of the sad things for the world that we don't know where he would've gone vocally."

"He was sort of sick from the cure," says Daniel Rey. "The chemo really kicked his ass. But he was feeling good for big chunks of time, and that's when we would work. It's a group of songs that Joey had gathered since the band broke up, and a few ideas he had before that, plus one cover song. And he was pretty precious about everything on it. We cut all the music, he was happy with it, and then we took our time and did the rest of the vocals."

"Those are songs that didn't make the first record," laughs Andy, concerning . . . *Ya Know?*. "They would have been demos that Ed Stasium took and had us do backing tracks to the vocals. And Ed did a very good job on that. Because they were not finished songs, finished arrangements. I think the drum tracks were done and I came in and overdubbed my bass parts."

"Wonderful and sad at the same time," recalls Richie Ramone, drummer on four . . . *Ya Know?* songs. "Those tracks were done, with all his singing and everything, to click tracks. So I had to listen to him singing in my ear as I practiced the songs, and then we went in the studio and I laid the drums over. It was tough. Hearing him over and over, right in your ear, brought back a lot of memories."

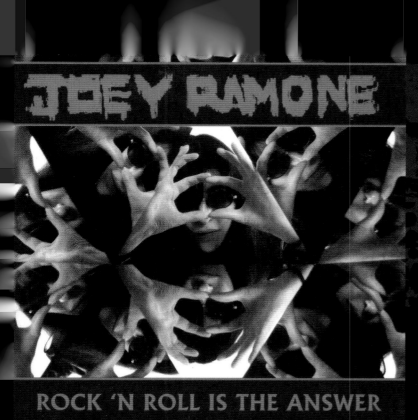

JOEY RAMONE

ROCK 'N ROLL IS THE ANSWER

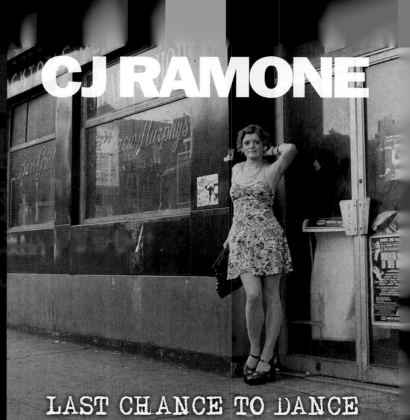

CJ RAMONE

LAST CHANCE TO DANCE

"TO ME, IT WAS VERY IMPORTANT THAT YOUNGER AUDIENCES GET TO CHECK OUT THE RAMONES, AND CJ ALLOWED THE OPPORTUNITY TO SEE AT LEAST A FACSIMILE OF THE RAMONES, WHICH WAS BETTER THAN NO RAMONES. AND THEY PUT ON A GREAT SHOW. I MEAN, IT WASN'T DEE DEE, BUT HE RESPECTED DEE DEE TREMENDOUSLY, AND TRIED TO BASICALLY STILL GIVE THEM AS MUCH DEE DEE AS HE COULD DO. SO UNDER THE CIRCUMSTANCES, IT TURNED OUT REAL GOOD ESPECIALLY FOR YOUNG FANS WHO'D NEVER SEEN THEM."

TOMMY RAMONE

"And Johnny said, 'CJ, you're an old fan. You want to see those guys because you're an old fan. The new fans haven't even seen Dee Dee or Tommy. It's like, they want to see you. You're good live. They want to see you on stage.' He said, 'Take your time and think about it and let me know what you want to do.' I went back to Johnny and said, 'All right, here's my terms. I'll do the tour. I'm not going to ride in a van. I'm gonna do it on my motorcycle. I don't want to do any interviews, I don't want to do any sound checks. I'm going to show up for the shows, play, and leave.' Johnny was like, 'All right, but if you miss a show, you miss a week's pay.' And a week's pay was $700. So I said, wow, big deal. So long."

"But when I thought about it, I realized that the Ramones deserved a better final tour than the one we had done in '95, which was playing the same little clubs that we had played every year. You know, nothing really special about it, no real fanfare, no press covering it, nobody coming out for it. And I realized that Lollapalooza was their last chance at a big tour. But it was also their last chance to understand what an impact they made. Because every band on that bill—Rancid, Soundgarden, Metallica— were fans of the Ramones when they were younger. And every day, all those different guys in all those different bands came over and hung out at the dressing room, and Johnny and Joey sat

there and held court. And it occurred to them, finally, what a huge influence they had on music. Those were all your biggest-selling bands of 1996 right there. And they were all coming over and just sitting there and staring at Johnny and Joey in awe and having great conversations."

Yet, true to form, the guys couldn't wrap up their twenty-year journey without one last squabble. CJ could see that Joey was struggling, even if Johnny might not have wanted to acknowledge it.

"He was just constantly uncomfortable. He was a big awkward guy and that's not an insult. So any medical thing at all really just made touring uncomfortable. You have to remember, we toured hard, and Joey really tried his best to keep up. But by the time 1996 came and we had announced the retirement tour and whatnot, at the end we actually had a $1 million offer to go down to South America. And Joey came to me at what was one of the last shows, possibly the last show, in L.A. He said, 'Hey, CJ, how would you feel if I turned down that offer in South America?' And I said to him, 'Joey, you gave them twenty-two years. You don't owe anybody anything at this point. You do what you think is best for you.' And that was what was best for him."

"Remember, I knew Joey was sick back in '94," continues CJ. "I found out that he was sick back then. So those last couple years were really tough.

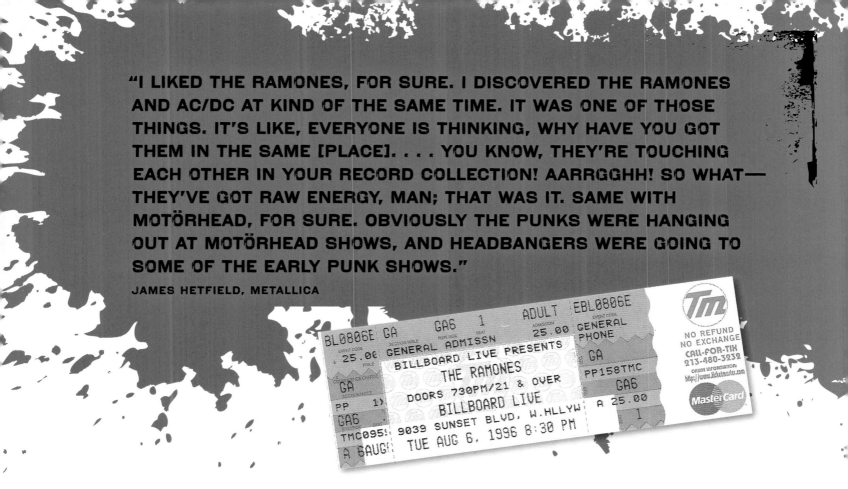

"I LIKED THE RAMONES, FOR SURE. I DISCOVERED THE RAMONES AND AC/DC AT KIND OF THE SAME TIME. IT WAS ONE OF THOSE THINGS. IT'S LIKE, EVERYONE IS THINKING, WHY HAVE YOU GOT THEM IN THE SAME [PLACE]. . . . YOU KNOW, THEY'RE TOUCHING EACH OTHER IN YOUR RECORD COLLECTION! AARRGGHH! SO WHAT— THEY'VE GOT RAW ENERGY, MAN; THAT WAS IT. SAME WITH MOTÖRHEAD, FOR SURE. OBVIOUSLY THE PUNKS WERE HANGING OUT AT MOTÖRHEAD SHOWS, AND HEADBANGERS WERE GOING TO SOME OF THE EARLY PUNK SHOWS."

JAMES HETFIELD, METALLICA

OPPOSITE: Joey at Lollapalooza. CJ Ramone on Joey: "The funny thing is that now, with a bit of historical context, Joey's probably got one of the most classic rock 'n' roll voices ever."

OPPOSITE, INSET: All access pass to the last show.

ABOVE: Lollapalooza was supposed to be their swan song, but their last gig was in the end a guest-studded affair at The Palace, which was recorded for Billboard Live (ticket stub above) and then subsequently documented for all time on the *We're Outta Here!* live album.

He wasn't at the top of his game when we retired by any stretch of the imagination, but he did his best to get through it. But yeah, this offer was two shows or something, in Argentina, a $1 million offer. Out of everybody in the band, I could've used it the most. You know, $250,000 is no small thing to turn down. But like I said, he was sick, he'd been doing it for twenty-two years, I'm not going to make him feel guilty for not wanting to do it. And not only that, I answered him as a friend, not as a business partner. I just answered him as a friend."

The Ramones' final show, a guest-studded affair at The Palace in L.A., August 6, 1996, would be immortalized through the live album, *We're Outta Here!*, issued November 18, 1997. It was a quick follow-up to the *Greatest Hits Live* record released June 18, 1996, built from a show at the Academy in New York on February 29, 1996—both are vast improvements over 1992's *Loco Live*.

"I don't think Marky was fine with it," says Rey, concerning the retirement in general. "You know, drummers, they're all about playing. They can't really sit back and strum their drums in their living room.

They have to be out there playing. Joey definitely needed a break mentally and physically, but he had mixed feelings too. And CJ was bummed because he was out of a gig."

"As for Johnny," he continues, "he just didn't want to be an old punk and look ridiculous up there. He wanted to leave like a boxer—on top. He wanted to move to California and collect posters and hang out with his friends and live the California Hollywood lifestyle. And it's a shame, because he was really doing it! And then he got sick. He bought a beautiful house with T-shirt money that he had stashed away, and he had cars and the Hollywood friends and swimming pool and he was living large."

"That was a great way to leave off," reflects CJ, "and it definitely never did get better. I remember seeing Joey on a couple of talk shows by himself, and I thought to myself, oh my God, he just looks lonely. When you're part of a unit like that that does something that really counts, and it's over with, it's a piece of you that is gone that nothing will ever take the place of. I'm not trying to compare playing music and touring the world to the sacrifice that people in the military

IT PROVED THAT WE WERE SPECIAL

THE RAMONES AND THE
ROCK AND ROLL HALL OF FAME

On March 18, 2002, the Ramones were inducted into the Rock and Roll Hall of Fame, at a ceremony at the Waldorf Astoria hotel in New York City. The acceptance speech membership consisted of Johnny, Marky, Tommy, and Dee Dee in a purple suit jacket and sassy black-dyed hair, with Mickey, Joey's brother, and his mom, Charlotte, also in attendance, and filmed for the touching occasion. As these things go, the line had to be drawn at CJ, with the bassist (who gets a thanks from Tommy), and Richie Ramone not being part of the ceremony.

The band was ushered in by Pearl Jam's Eddie Vedder, sporting a Mohawk, a black leather jacket, and a Ramones T-shirt, along with the biggest punk band of the time, Green Day, who celebrated the event with performances of "Teenage Lobotomy," "Rockaway Beach," and "Blitzkrieg Bop."

"It was wonderful; it proved that we were special," reflected Tommy. "Some people get in based on the fact that they sell a lot of records. So obviously for a group like the Ramones to get in, it has to be special. It was a great honor. It meant that we were recognized as an innovative and important band. So I think that meant probably more to us than it might have to some other artists who got in. As far as whether I felt it would be possible for us to get in? Well, call

me deluded or whatever, but I always felt that if anybody belonged in the Rock and Roll Hall of Fame, it was the Ramones. Was I surprised that we got in on the first ballot? Oh yeah. The chances of that, I think, were remote. That was really mind-boggling."

Tommy also admitted that seeing everybody again was "bizarre. The thing with the Ramones, especially near the end, was that any kind of interaction was just so strange. They just kept getting stranger and stranger, I guess, at the end. When people don't communicate, they form different camps. Then when it comes to situations like the Rock and Roll Hall of Fame, it causes a disadvantage. And actually this didn't only happen with the Ramones. The Talking Heads weren't talking to each other either. It happens in most bands actually. Touring is not a positive thing for future friendships. It puts a lot of strain on best friends. Look what just happened with Mick and Keith. Mick's knighted or whatever, and Keith is talking like it's nothing—that's understandable. But yeah, it puts a lot of strain on friends, and they often go their own way."

Impressively, as Tommy indicates, the Ramones were inducted in their first year of eligibility, reflecting their lofty position in pop culture, but more pointedly their fit and

adjacency to the Hall's notoriously debated biases—being punks from New York that were also critics' darlings frankly worked in their favor. There was no hint of ungratefulness or derision from any of the guys as they accepted, even though Dee Dee irreverently but endearingly thanked himself and no one else, and ticked the band off by not showing up in uniform. In fact, Tommy went so far as to say that the honor would have meant everything to Joey. This was not Kiss or the Sex Pistols—the Ramones played by their own rules, were comfortable in their skin, and took the induction for what it was: validation.

In keeping with the "awkward" nature of almost anything to do with the band, Joey's award sat unclaimed and abandoned on the podium as the guys ended their brief (and awkward) speeches and scrambled for cover. To their credit, the Hall of Fame re-bestowed his award seven years later, Tommy and Mickey accepting on Joey's behalf at the hands of Hall president Joel Peresman and legendary first manager of the band, Danny Fields.

TOP: Dee Dee breaks ranks with his jacket, but makes good by charming the crowd with his goofy and succinct self-congratulating acceptance speech.

BOTTOM: The industry balked at first at the idea of situating the Rock Hall in Cleveland, but over the years, the venue has proven itself an eventful and substantial tourist attraction for this city on the rebound.

make, but to me, it's similar. Guys who go to war and fight together, when it's all over with, they're lost. They're lost when they don't have their team around them anymore. And I really think that's what Joey was feeling after it was all over."

After the band dissipated, fate would rain down on the Ramones mercilessly, cementing their legend as American icons much like James Dean and Marilyn Monroe. Except, typically, the end of the Ramones was comparatively messy and ragged, if no less tragic, given the scope of the mortality expressed. Dee Dee Ramone would die of a heroin overdose June 5, 2002—three months after holding court at the Rock and Roll Hall of Fame when the Ramones were inducted. Johnny Ramone passed away from prostate cancer that got him on September 15, 2004. Then on July 11, 2014, Tommy Ramone died from bile duct cancer.

But Joey would be the first to go, succumbing to lymphoma in 2001, a fate that perhaps was avoidable. "December is when he fell," explains Andy Shernoff. "Late December, he went out for a walk and he slipped on the ice, in the East Village. The cancer medicine makes your bones soft, and so he broke his hip when he fell. A normal person might've fallen and might not have broken a hip. But to treat the broken hip, they had to take him off the cancer medicine, and when they did that, his cancer came back quite strong, so he didn't last long—he died on April 15. And I was actually in the room when he passed. I watched him take his last breath. But that fall is basically what killed him."

"He was in bed; he was unconscious," he continues. "And as it looked like he was fading away, his brother put on 'In a Little While,' a U2 song. Bono said that the song was elevated by Joey's death. It talks about the pain

On the magazine cover:

FREE CD!

CLAPTON
Layla Revisited

FELA KUTI
African Soul Rebel

MOJO
music magazine

RADIOHEAD! PAUL SIMON! & MORE!
33 PAGES OF REVIEWS

JOEY
10 YEARS GONE...

RAMONES

INSIDE!
MAGAZINE
BOOTSY
COLLINS
THE LOW ANTHEM
THE UNTHANKS
ARETHA
FRANKLIN
SOUNDGARDEN
ROBBIE
ROBERTSON

PLUS!
GUNS.
DRUGS.
POP!
When Phil Spector
Met New York Punk...

FOO FIGHTERS
Backstage At Their
Secret Show

BEADY EYE
Liam's Live Return!

If your CD is missing please
inform your newsagent.
For copyright reasons the
CD is not available in some
overseas territories.

MAY 2011 £4.50   US$9.99   CAN$13.50

ABOVE LEFT: Tommy Ramone, as part of the "Joey Ramone Birthday Bashers," performs at the Joey Ramone Birthday Bash 2007 at The Fillmore New York at Irving Plaza on May 19, 2007. Upon Johnny's death in 2004, Tommy was, for ten years, the last surviving member of the original Ramones, becoming the third member to die from cancer, succumbing in 2014 at the age of 65.

ABOVE RIGHT: A May 2011 *Mojo* cover. The Ramones will forever be the subject of periodic press retrospectives.

PAGES 202-203: The original Ramones on January 31, 1978.

of a hangover going away. And Mickey put the song on, on a boombox in the room, just before he died. It was Mickey; Mickey's wife Arlene; it was Arturo; it was Joey's mom Charlotte; and Charlotte's boyfriend at the time, a guy named Larry; and me. And that was it; it was just those people.

The cancer didn't kill him, or it didn't kill him for another six years. He was getting better, and in 2000, he was ready to do some shows. He was definitely feeling better. So it was just some very, very bad luck by slipping on some ice, that really killed him."

With Tommy's passing, the entirety of the original Ramones was no more, which has got to be some sort of morbid world record. Nonetheless, it is at least heartening that one of their last awkward career moves had laced around it some manner of silver lining.

"Like I say, in the end, that Lollapalooza tour was nice because I think that's when they finally

understood how important they were," agrees CJ in closing. "Because in their minds, never having achieved that golden dream of commercial success, and platinum records and having their own private plane, that really bothered them. But it's not like they died poor. These guys did not die poor. And in their hearts, they knew how great they were, but still they just could not accept the fact that they were ignored for all those years. It really bothered them. And I told Johnny that a bunch of times. I said, you guys can't measure your success by your record sales. You guys measure your success by the people, the bands and the music scene that you've influenced. You influenced everybody—everybody! There isn't a band that we've been on tour with or that you're going to read about that doesn't list the Ramones as an influence. And that's your legacy. That's what you're going to leave behind."

Discography

Ramones (February 1976)
Produced by Craig Leon
Side 1: 1. Blitzkrieg Bop (2:12)
2. Beat on the Brat (2:30) 3. Judy Is
a Punk (1:30) 4. I Wanna Be Your
Boyfriend (2:24). 5. Chain Saw (1:55)
6. Now I Wanna Sniff Some Glue (1:34)
7. I Don't Wanna Go Down to the
Basement (2:35)
Side 2: 1. Loudmouth (2:14) 2. Havana
Affair (2:00) 3. Listen to My Heart
(1:56) 4. 53rd & 3rd (2:19) 5. Let's
Dance (1:51) 6. I Don't Wanna Walk
Around with You (1:43) 7. Today Your
Love, Tomorrow the World (2:09)
Notes: Joey Ramone: vocals; Johnny
Ramone: guitar; Dee Dee Ramone: bass;
Tommy Ramone: drums.

Leave Home (January 1977)
Produced by Tony Bongiovi and
Tommy Erdelyi
Side 1: 1. Glad to See You Go (2:10)
2. Gimme, Gimme Shock Treatment (1:38)
3. I Remember You (2:15) 4. Oh, Oh, I
Love Her So (2:03) 5. Carbona Not Glue
(1:56) 6. Suzy Is a Headbanger (2:08)
7. Pinhead (2:42)
Side 2: 1. Now I Wanna Be a Good Boy
(2:10) 2. Swallow My Pride (2:03)
3. What's Your Game (2:33)
4. California Sun (1:58). 5. Commando
(1:51) 6. You're Gonna Kill That Girl
(2:36) 7. You Should Never Have Opened
That Door (1:54)
Notes: Joey Ramone: vocals; Johnny
Ramone: guitar; Dee Dee Ramone: bass;
Tommy Ramone: drums.

Rocket to Russia (November 1977)
Produced by Tony Bongiovi and
Tommy Erdelyi
Side 1: 1. Cretin' Hop (1:55)
2. Rockaway Beach (2:06) 3. Here
Today, Gone Tomorrow (2:47) 4. Locket
Love (2:09). 5. I Don't Care (1:38)
6. Sheena Is a Punk Rocker (2:49)
7. We're a Happy Family (2:47)
Side 2: 1. Teenage Lobotomy (2:00)
2. Do You Wanna Dance? (1:52)
3. I Wanna Be Well (2:28) 4. I Can't
Give You Anything (1:57). 5. Ramona
(2:35) 6. Surfin' Bird (2:37) 7. Why Is
It Always this Way? (2:32)
Notes: Joey Ramone: vocals; Johnny
Ramone: guitar; Dee Dee Ramone: bass;
Tommy Ramone: drums.

Road to Ruin (September 1978)
Produced by Tommy Erdelyi and
Ed Stasium
Side 1: 1. I Just Want to Have
Something to Do (2:42) 2. I Wanted
Everything (3:18) 3. Don't Come Close
(2:44) 4. I Don't Want You (2:26)
5. Needles and Pins (2:21) 6. I'm
Against It (2:07)
Side 2: 1. I Wanna Be Sedated (2:29)
2. Go Mental (2:42) 3. Questioningly
(3:22) 4. She's the One (2:13) 5. Bad
Brain (2:25) 6. It's a Long Way Back
(2:20)
Notes: Drums: Tommy Ramone is replaced
by Marky Ramone.

End of the Century (February 1980)
Produced by Phil Spector
Side 1: 1. Do You Remember Rock 'n'
Roll Radio? (3:50) 2. I'm Affected
(2:51) 3. Danny Says (3:06) 4. Chinese
Rock (2:28) 5. The Return of Jackie
and Judy (3:12) 6. Let's Go (2:31)
Side 2: 1. Baby, I Love You (3:47)
2. I Can't Make It on Time (2:32)
3. This Ain't Havana (2:18) 4. Rock 'n'
Roll High School (2:38) 5. All the Way
(2:29) 6. High Risk Insurance (2:08)
Notes: Drums: Tommy Ramone is replaced
by Marky Ramone.

Pleasant Dreams (July 1981)
Produced by Graham Gouldman
Side 1: 1. We Want the Airwaves (3:22)
2. All's Quiet on the Eastern Front
(2:14) 3. The KKK Took My Baby Away
(2:32) 4. Don't Go (2:48) 5. You Sound
Like You're Sick (2:42) 6. It's Not My
Place (in the 9 to 5 World) (3:24)
Side 2: 1. She's a Sensation (3:29)
2. 7-11 (3:38) 3. You Didn't Mean
Anything to Me (3:00) 4. Come on Now
(2:33) 5. This Business Is Killing Me
(2:41) 6. Sitting in My Room (2:30)
Notes: Drums: Tommy Ramone is replaced
by Marky Ramone.

Subterranean Jungle (February 1983)
Produced by Ritchie Cordell and
Glen Kolotkin
Side 1: 1. Little Bit O' Soul (2:43)
2. I Need Your Love (3:03) 3. Outsider
(2:10) 4. What'd Ya Do? (2:24)
5. Highest Trails Above (2:09)
6. Somebody Like Me (2:34)
Side 2: 1. Psycho Therapy (2:35)
2. Time Has Come Today (4:25) 3. My-My
Kind of a Girl (3:31) 4. In the Park
(2:34) 5. Time Bomb (2:09) 6. Every
Time I Eat Vegetables It Makes Me
Think of You (3:04)
Notes: Drums: Tommy Ramone is replaced
by Marky Ramone.

Too Tough to Die (October 1984)
Produced by Tommy Erdelyi and
Ed Stasium
Side 1: 1. Mama's Boy (2:09) 2. I'm Not
Afraid of Life (3:12) 3. Too Tough to
Die (2:35) 4. Durango 95 (0:55)
5. Wart Hog (1:54) 6. Danger Zone
(2:03) 7. Chasing the Night (4:25)
Side 2: 1. Howling at the Moon (Sha La
La) (4:06) 2. Daytime Dilemma (Dangers
of Love) (4:31) 3. Planet Earth 1988
(2:54) 4. Humankind (2:41) 5. Endless
Vacation (1:45) 6. No Go (3:03)
Notes: Drums: Marky Ramone is replaced
by Richie Ramone.

Animal Boy (May 1986)
Produced by Jean Beauvoir
Side 1: 1. Somebody Put Something in My
Drink (3:23) 2. Animal Boy (1:50)
3. Love Kills (2:19) 4. Apeman Hop
(2:02) 5. She Belongs to Me (3:54)
6. Crummy Stuff (2:06)
Side 2: 1. My Brain Is Hanging Upside
Down (Bonzo Goes to Bitburg) (3:55)
2. Mental Hell (2:38) 3. Eat That Rat
(1:37) 4. Freak of Nature (1:32)
5. Hair of the Dog (2:19) 6. Something
to Believe In (4:09)
Notes: Drums: Marky Ramone is replaced
by Richie Ramone.

Halfway to Sanity (September 1987)
Produced by the Ramones and Daniel Rey
Side 1: 1. I Wanna Live (2:36) 2. Bop
'Til You Drop (2:09) 3. Garden of
Serenity (2:35) 4. Weasel Face (1:49)
5. Go Lil' Camaro Go (2:00) 6. I Know
Better Now (2:37)
Side 2: 1. Death of Me (2:39) 2. I Lost
My Mind (1:33) 3. A Real Cool Time
(2:38) 4. I'm Not Jesus (2:52) 5. Bye
Bye Baby (4:33) 6. Worm Man (1:52)
Notes: Drums: Marky Ramone is replaced
by Richie Ramone.

Brain Drain (March 1989)
Produced by Bill Laswell
Side 1: 1. I Believe in Miracles (3:19)
2. Zero Zero UFO (2:25) 3. Don't Bust
My Chops (2:28) 4. Punishment Fits the
Crime (3:05) 5. All Screwed Up (3:59)
6. Pallisades Park (2:22)
Side 2: 1. Pet Sematary (3:30) 2. Learn
to Listen (1:50) 3. Can't Get You
Outta My Mind (3:21) 4. Ignorance Is
Bliss (2:38) 5. Come Back, Baby (4:01)
6. Merry Christmas (I Don't Want to
Fight Tonight) (2:04)
Notes: Drums: Richie Ramone is replaced
by the returning Marky Ramone. "Pet
Sematary" is produced by Jean Beauvoir
and Daniel Rey.

Mondo Bizarro (September 1992)
Produced by Ed Stasium
Side 1: 1. Censorshit (3:13) 2. The Job
That Ate My Brain (2:17) 3. Poison
Heart (4:04) 4. Anxiety (2:04)
5. Strength to Endure (2:59) 6. It's
Gonna Be Alright (3:20) 7. Take It As
It Comes (2:07) 8. Main Man (3:29)
9. Tomorrow She Goes Away (2:41)
10. I Won't Let It Happen (2:22)
11. Cabbies on Crack (3:01) 12. Heidi
Is a Headcase (2:57) 13. Touring (2:51)
Notes: Bassist/vocalist: Dee Dee Ramone
is replaced by CJ Ramone. This is the
first Ramones album of the CD era.

Acid Eaters (March 1994)
Produced by Scott Hackwith
Side 1: 1. Journey to the Center of the
Mind (2:52) 2. Substitute (3:15)
3. Out of Time (2:41) 4. The Shape of
Things to Come (1:46) 5. Somebody to
Love (2:31) 6. When I Was Young (3:16)
7. 7 and 7 Is (1:50) 8. My Back Pages
(2:27) 9. Can't Seem to Make You Mine
(2:42) 10. Have You Ever Seen the
Rain? (2:22) 11. I Can't Control
Myself (2:55) 12. Surf City (2:26)
Notes: Covers album, originally slated
to be a covers EP.

¡Adios Amigos! (July 1995)
Produced by Daniel Rey
Side 1: 1. I Don't Want to Grow Up
(2:43) 2. Makin' Monsters for My
Friends (2:33) 3. It's Not for Me to
Know (2:50) 4. The Crusher (2:24)
5. Life's a Gas (3:35) 6. Take the
Pain Away (2:40) 7. I Love You (2:21)
8. Cretin Family (2:08) 9. Have a Nice
Day (1:41) 10. Scattergun (2:30)
11. Got Alot to Say (1:42) 12. She
Talks to Rainbows (3:13) 13. Born to
Die in Berlin (3:31)

Sources

LIVE ALBUMS

It's Alive (April 1979)
Loco Live (March 1992)
Greatest Hits Live (June 1996)
We're Outta Here (November 1997)
You Don't Come Close (May 2001)
King Biscuit Flower Hour: NYC 1978
  (August 2003)
Live on Air (February 2010)

COMPILATIONS

Ramones Mania (May 1988)
All the Stuff (and More) Volume One
  (May 1990)
All the Stuff (and More) Volume Two
  (May 1990)
Anthology (July 1999)
Ramones Mania 2 (April 2000)
Masters of Rock (August 2001)
Best of the Chrysalis Years (May 2002)
The Chrysalis Years (August 2002)
Loud, Fast Ramones: Their Toughest Hits
  (October 2002)
The Best of the Ramones (May 2004)
Weird Tales of the Ramones
  (August 2005)
Greatest Hits (June 2006)
Essential (July 2007)
Rockaway Beach (August 2007)

SOLO ALBUMS

Qualification for listing is essentially
  solo album "by name."

CJ Ramone — *Reconquista* (June 2012
  digital; June 2013 on CD and LP)
CJ Ramone — *Last Chance to Dance*
  (November 2014)
Dee Dee King — *Standing in the
  Spotlight* (December 1989)
Dee Dee Ramone — *I Hate Freaks Like You*
  (June 1994)
Dee Dee Ramone — *Zonked!* (October 1997;
  titled *Ain't It Fun* in Europe)
Dee Dee Ramone — *Hop Around*
  (January 2000)
Dee Dee Ramone — *Greatest & Latest*
  (June 2000)
Joey Ramone — *Don't Worry About Me*
  (February 2002)
Joey Ramone — *. . . Ya Know?* (May 2012)
Marky Ramone and the Intruders — *Marky
  Ramone & The Intruders* (1996)
Marky Ramone and the Intruders — *The
  Answer to Your Problems?* (July 1999;
  titled *Don't Blame Me* in South
  America)
Marky Ramone and the SpeedKings — *No
  If's, And's or But's!* (November 2001;
  issued in the USA as *Legends Bleed* in
  October 2002)
Marky Ramone and the SpeedKings — *Alive*
  (September 2002)
Marky Ramone — *Start of the Century*
  (March 2006)
Richie Ramone — *Entitled* (October 2013)

The author would like to thank the following people for allowing him to interview them: Ralph Alfonso, Ron Asheton, Roberta Bayley, Jean Beauvoir, Tony Bongiovi, Michael Davis, George DuBose, Graham Gouldman, Scott Hackwith, Flo Hayler, John Holmstrom, Lenny Kaye, Jari-Pekka Laitio-Ramone, Bill Laswell, Craig Leon, CJ Ramone, Marky Ramone, Richie Ramone, Daniel Rey, Andy Shernoff, Syl Sylvain, and Tony Wright.

Additional author's archive quotes are courtesy of: Cheetah Chrome, Jeff "Mono Mann" Conolly, Lita Ford, James Hetfield, Matt Mahurin, Jonathan Poneman, Ross the Boss, Pete Shelley, Dave Vanian, Tony Wright, and Billy Zoom.

ADDITIONAL SOURCES
PERIODICALS

Alfonso, Ralph. "The Ramones." *Cheap Thrills*, April 1977.
——. "The Ramones." *Crash 'n' Burn News*, June 1977.
Bangs, Lester. "Ramones Go Depresso!" *Trouser Press*, November 1978.
Barbieri, Kelly. "Hey Ho They're Gonna Go!" *Live Wire*, Aug/Sept 1995.
Bidini, Dave. "Ramones: The Band Who Build a Miracle." *Shades*, Oct/Nov 1979.
Billboard. "They're Still Ramones After All These Years." March 26, 1983.
Bomp. "*Road to Ruin*: Review." January 1979.
Cohen, Mitch. "What Price Glory? Ramones Soldier On." *Creem*, June 1980.
Coon, Carolyn. "*Glad to See You Go*: Review." *Melody Maker*, February 19, 1977.
Devenish, Colin. "Johnny Ramone Stays Tough." *Rolling Stone*, June 24, 2002.
Ehm, Erica. "Interview with the Ramones." *New Music*, September 1987.
Fricke, David. "Rock & Roll H.S.——The Ramones Liven Up a Light Summer Movie." *Circus*, July 10, 1979.
——. "*It's Alive*: Review." *Trouser Press*, August 1979.
——. "*Pleasant Dreams*: Review." *Rolling Stone*, October 29, 1981.
Gomes, Al. "Ramones Get Back the Spirit." *Providence Local*, April 1984.
Gordon, Keith A. "Ramones Redux." *Metro*, May 1990.
Green, Jim. "Ramones Finished High School." *Trouser Press*, July 1979.
Hammond, Kathy. "Record Ranting: Ramones." *Twisted*, 1977.
Hit Parader. "The Ramones in Their Own Words." October 1981.
Holmstrom, John. "Ramones." *Punk*, March 1976.
Isler, Scott. "*Road to Ruin*: Review." *Trouser Press*, November 1978.
——. "*Subterranean Jungle*: Review." *Trouser Press*, June 1983.
Kaye, Don. "The Ramones." *Rip*, April 1993.
Kinsella, Warren. "The Ramones: A Perfect Rock Group?" *Music Express*, May 1980.
Lamont, John. "*Rocket to Russia*: Review." *Stage Life*, February 1978.

Loder, Kurt. "*End of the Century*: Review." *Rolling Stone*, March 20, 1980.
Milner, Greg. "Ramones Come Home." *Spin*, May 2001.
Strick, Wesley. "Ramones! Leather Boys in Bondage." *Gig*, January 1977.
Trouser Press (Vol.6, No.12, author unknown). "22 For the '80s: Prognostication by the Usual Gang of Idiots." January 1980.
Zeller, Craig. "Are You Ready For Ramonamania?" *Hit Parader*, April 1978.

BOOKS

Holmstrom, John. "Rock 'n' Roll High School: The Movie That Will Go Down in History!" from *Punk: The Best of "Punk Magazine*." New York: *Punk Magazine*/ Harper Collins, 2012.
Kent, Nick. *Apathy for the Devil*. London: Faber and Faber, 2010.
Savage, Jon. *Time Travel: From the Sex Pistols to Nirvana*. Random House. 1996.
Shires, Glenn. "Interview with Dee Dee Ramone at E.J.'s, Portland, Oregon." January 19, 2000.

ONLINE AND BROADCAST INTERVIEWS

Kill, Pam. [OR Kihl?] "Interview with Johnny Ramone and Dee Dee Ramone." *The Ramones RAW*, 1983. www.youtube. com/2LkYsbc1yXw
Laitio-Ramone, Jarri-Pekka. Various interviews; www.ramonesheaven.com.
Prindle, Mark. Various interviews; markprindle.com.
Raw & Uncut. "Interview with Joey Ramone and Dee Dee Ramone." 1986. www.youtube.com/FnjQo9hhiOY
Richen, John. "Interview with Johnny Ramone." Smokebox.net, December 1984.

Index

All images are denoted in **bold**

Picture credits

With grateful thanks to all the archives and individuals who have contributed to this book. Record sleeves reproduced courtesy of Bertelsmann, DC-Jam Records, Fat Wreck Chords, Philips Records, and Sire Records (Warner Music Group).

Front cover: (r) © Vintage Photos/Alamy (l) © Roberta Bayley via Alamy
Alamy: © AF Archive/Alamy: 82; © CBW/Alamy: 118, 142l; © DPA Picture Alliance/Alamy: 13bl; © Granamour Weems Collection/Alamy: 143l; © Interfoto/Alamy: 149r; © Richard Levine: 200r; © Paul Natkin: 6; © Stephen Parker: 144; © Pictorial Press: 75, 86, 90; Jeff Morgan: 40l; © Mick Sinclair: 35, 43 inset top, © Tracks Images: 13 inset; © Ioannis Tsouratsis: 102, 103; © Vintage Photos: 2/3; © Zuma Press: 163
Ralph Alfonso: © Ralph Alfonso: 41b, 93b
Beinecke Library, Yale University: © Roberta Bayley: 43, 48; © John Holmstrom archive: 49
Corbis: © Hiroyuki Matsumoto/Corbis: 25b; © Steve Jennings/Corbis: 170
Kevin Estrada: © Kevin Estrada: 184, 196
Danny Fields: © Danny Fields: 42
Chris Forssblad: © Chris Forssblad: 42 inset, 53, 59l, 59c, 59r, 95r, 97l, 104, 120bl, 120tr, 12, 124, 125l, 125c, 129, 137l, 138b, 140, 147l, 147c, 147r, 149tl, 149bl, 154r, 182
Frank White Photography: © Kevin Hodapp/Frank White: 89; © Bob Leafe/Frank

White: 99; Frank White/Frank White: 157
Richard Galbraith: © Richard Galbraith: 77, 78/9
Mike Gerrish: © Mike Gerrish: 57r
Getty Images: © Roberta Bayley: 11, 17tr, 18, 30, 37t, 37b, 41t, 70, 73, 74, 76; © Bob Berg: 195; © FilmMagic/Jeff Kravitz: 180; © Dick Halstead: 137r; Dave Hogan: 112; © Hulton Archive/Getty Images: 13t; © Tim Mosenfelder: 188; *New York Daily News* Archive via Getty Images: 164, 2001; © Brian Rasic: 108; Tim Roney: 128, © SSSPL: 111; © *Toronto Star*/Keith Beaty via Getty Images: 167r; © Ullsteinbild/Jazz Archive Hamburg: 173; © Mark Weiss: 179
Getty Images/Archive Photos: © Frank Edwards: 951
Getty Images Entertainment: © Larry Busacca: 183; © Ray Tamarra: 2011; © Michael Ochs Archive/Getty Images: 15; Larry Hulst: 114, 123; Richard McCaffrey: 14
Getty Images Images/Redferns: © Richard E. Aaron: 28; © Brian Cooke: 68; © Ian Dickson: 8, 32, 56, 62/3; © Erica Eichenberg: 44/5; © GAB Archive/Getty Images: 1, 39; © Mick Hutson: 158; © Bob King: 148; Robert Knight Archive/Getty Images: 187; MAI/Lex Van Rossen: 46/7; Peter Pakvis: 146, 161; © Ed Perlstein: 117, 202/3; © Ebet Roberts: 21, 25t, 67, 81, 101, 185; © Gus Stewart: 17tl, 72; © Gary Wolstoneholme: 152

Getty Images/WireImage: © RJ Capak: 199t; © Jeffrey Mayer: 135; © Kevin Mazur: 165; © Frank Mullen: 119; © Patti Oudekirk: 191b; Sean Sabhasaigh: 1671
Bobby Grossman: © Bobby Grossman: 40r
Bob Gruen: © Bob Gruen: 26/7, 29, 31
Flickr: 17b, 38
iStockphoto: 199b
The Kobal Collection: © MGM: 52; © New World: 85; © Warner Bros./Hawk Films: 122
Lucius Books, York: (luciusbooks.com): 49t
Photoshot: © Barry Schultz/Sunshine: 69
Martin Popoff: 54, 61, 97r
Private Collection: 20, 58, 81r, 81 inset top, 83, 91, 94, 1261, 138t, 141t,142r, 162, 175l, 192, 193tl, 193tr, 201r, 143r
Don Pyle: © Don Pyle: 92, 93tl, 93tr
Jari-Pekka Laitio Ramone: 168, 169l, 169r
Richie Ramone: (Mozzchopz): © Richie Ramone: 193b
Rex Shutterstock: © Peter Mazel/Sunshine: 64
Gaston Sanchez/Ramonesforever.com: 23, 25 inset, 55, 57l, 1131, 113r, 126r, 132, 141br, 144 inset, 151l, 151r, 154l, 156l, 157 inset, 166, 177l, 177r, 191t, 196
Topfoto: © Allen Tannenbaum/Imageworks: 136; © Photoshot: 106/7; © Ullsteinbild: 105
Paul Wright: 76 inset; © Mark Perry 124

Key: b = bottom, c = center, l = left, r = right, t = top

Acknowledgments

The author would like to thank Will Steeds and Laura Ward at Elephant Book Company for their enthusiasm for this project and making it happen, as well as Barbara Berger at Sterling Publishing who championed the project from conception to completion, and whose passion and expertise shaped it into the book before you. The author and Elephant would also like to thank the following people at Sterling Publishing: creative director Jo Obarowski, interior art director Chris Thompson, cover art director Elizabeth Mihaltse, and production director Fred Pagan.

Grateful thanks go to Jo de Vries for charting the project through the publishing process in the UK. Thank you also to

Sally Claxton for her dogged picture research, which unearthed some fantastic images. Many thanks go to Paul Palmer-Edwards at Grade Design for the incredible artwork and design he has produced for the book, which adds just the right amount of original punk chaos to please any Ramones fan.

A final thank-you must again go to all those who have allowed me to reproduce their interviews, reviews, and other words of wisdom on these pages, alongside those who took time out of their busy lives to submit themselves to my fan-boy interrogations— I only hope they will feel that this is a worthy celebration of the first, the best, the brudders, at forty years of appreciated influence and counting.